Cloth Diapers

The ultimate guide to textiles, washing, & more.

written and illustrated by

Bailey Bouwman

Cloth Diaper Podcast
bailey@clothdiaperpodcast.com

www.clothdiaperpodcast.com

What's New In the 2021 Update

I started this book in 2019. I published it with errors in the Spring of 2020, and sent it to the printers with the same errors. I removed products no longer available (best of my knowledge) and updated information based on new findings and experiences. New photos were also added. Cloth diapering is always in flux.

I want to thank Jocelyn Gibson-Keener
for supporting me in editing the 2021 version.

Disclaimer

Acknowledgements

I am the person I am because the cloth diaper community mentored and loved me over the past 5 years.

I am thankful for the What To Expect website, where I met women like Jaimie P., a mom of two on the East Coast. Jaimie collected and shared information about cloth diapers on this forum. She is the first person I learnt from, and from her I met many other amazing women. Today, these moms are the Chewy Granola Moms and they are my everything.

I am thankful for Suzi S., for helping me learn how to blog. From a crash course in SEO to connecting me with brands and retailers, Suzi was influential in shaping my passion for local shopping, responsible consumerism, and more.

I am thankful for my husband, Eric. He encouraged me to write this book. I started it as a 20 page document in Canva in the spring of my first bunion surgery. Here it is today, as 200+ pages of diaper information. Eric has always been my champion, giving me the tools and space to create cloth diaper content for over 4 years. He bought my first camera, mic, and book.

And for you, the cloth diaper community. There are countless influencers, bloggers, creators, and moms on Instagram and Facebook who rally around me. I am grateful for conversations we have, the emails in my inbox, and the people I meet in the grocery store.
Thank You.

Word from the Author, 2021

I am absolutely blown away by the support that I have recieved in publishing this book last year. This book sold over 125 paper copies and over 300 digital copies within the first year. So many bloggers, brands, and retailers have reached out in support and I hope with all my heart that we can get this book to wholesale as a quick start guide to empower and support the cloth diaper community.

I know you have a choice when it comes to learning about cloth diapering and I am incredibly blessed and grateful that you have choosen to support me and learn from me. I hope that you find me on social media, and continue to be a positive change in the cloth diaper community.

We can make cloth diapering mainstream. It just requires cooperation, collaboration and the goodness of our hearts to recoginze that we need to support families. I hope to find the time this year to write another book sharing all the things that you don't need to know to cloth diaper. And if you catch a spelling mistake, I hope that you remember we are all human and spelling is not a reflection of their worth. Spelling is a privilege, and we all make mistakes. But your girl is self-published and without the budget of an editor.

And don't forget to try out my Cloth Diaper Quiz online to find out what type of diaper is best for your family https://www.clothdiaperpodcast.com/cloth-diaper-quiz/

TABLE OF CONTENTS

INTRODUCTION

Thank you for purchasing this book on how to cloth diaper. I want this guide to help you be confident in cloth diapering. This isn't about the one best way to diaper, but a guide to help you find a way that works for your family.

You will find information that disagrees with this book. That is okay. I'm not here to create a fight or war on the right way to cloth diaper. I share with you my experience and learnings as an member of the cloth diaper community and podcast host over the past five years. This information is not wrong. It is one perspective from one experience.

The cloth diaper space can get heated.
Choose to be kind and considerate.
Choose the information that works for you.
Don't hate on the information that doesn't.
Talk about cloth diapering from your experience and don't infer that your experience is the only experience.

If you're looking for stories of cloth diapering told by other parents, check out my podcast on Apple Podcast, Podbean, Spotify and YouTube - Cloth Diaper Podcast. I chat with parents about what worked or didn't work for their family.

There will be questions.
There will be many more questions.
There will be hiccups, problems, and stumbles.
But, you got this.

We are here for you.

THIS IS YOUR STORY.
THIS IS YOUR JOURNEY IN MOTHERHOOD.

You can be who want to be.
You can do what you want to do.

You can purchase cloth diaper clothing from
clothdiaperpodcast.shop

My Cloth Diaper Journey

It's important to know where I started. You don't have to read this section but if you are curious on a mini life biography of why I am who I am, and why I continue to cloth diaper and support the community. This is the section to read.

I always knew I would cloth diaper. My parents cloth diapered. I hold a degree in Environmental Studies. I use reusable feminine hygiene products for the health of my skin. Cloth Diapering was the next step. The struggle was that I knew about cloth diapering. But I didn't know how to cloth diaper. I had to learn how to cloth diaper. Just like you. And to do so, I scoured the internet.

My first cloth diaper purchase was on Boxing Day 2014 *(a Canadian post-Christmas shopping sale),* I ordered my first stash of cloth diapers: 24 Bummis cotton prefolds in a size 2, along with an assortment of covers (size 1 Bummis, Newborn Blueberry Capri, Size 1 AppleCheeks). This was a great starter stash, but my 8lb baby doubled his birth weight in 6 weeks. Newborn diapers and size 1 covers, just didn't cut

My first stash shot, September 2015

1 week old, first diaper. Failed Jelly roll prefold with a size 1 Blueberry Capri cover.

it anymore. I ordered one size diapers from Canadian cloth diaper retailers, and quickly built a new stash. I tried a little of everything.

- The first diaper I got rid of was the bumGenius FreeTime. *I didn't like the bulk of microfibre on this All In One diaper.*
- The first diaper I fell in love with was a Blueberry Simplex. *It fit my chunky monkey, and was FINALLY absorbent enough.*

In 2015, Facebook groups existed, but they were not on my radar. I joined *www.whattoexpect.com* and found my cloth diapering people - where I posted my first fluff mail, participated in daily OTB threads *(on the bum, where we posted pictures of our kids in diapers)*, and learnt everything about cloth diapering. This fueled the early days of my addiction and enthusiasim for cloth diapering.

Facebook Groups became more popular and our small forum-based community moved to Facebook. We called the group *Our Cloth Diaper Addiction,* and learnt more about cloth diapering and dreamt of becoming a mentor and leader in the cloth diaper space. I also met my best friends in motherhood. We are all still friends in an amazing new community where we talk about Kindergarten, new babies, and the ever evolving challenges of our lives including the pandemic of COVID-19.

Motherhood was the start of a new blog - *SimplyMomBailey* - a space to share my journey in motherhood, the things I did, and things I wanted to do. Local cloth diaper blogger, Suzi from *ClothDiaperAddicts,* helped me grow this platform through her advice as a writer and blogger. This blog still exists and you will find many links to original reviews and cloth diaper content.

This blog encouraged cloth diapering to become a hobby. I bought diapers just review them. I tried to connect with brands and retailers but that didn't work out like it does for other people. The lack of brand sponsorships didn't stop me. I still continued to review diapers and talk about diapers. I love writing; I love talking about cloth diapering; and I love sharing stories.

My first big brand relationship was when I was selected as a Brand Ambassador for Omaiki, a Quebec cloth diaper brand. This was one of the most exciting moments of my cloth diaper blogger career. Being ambassador is one of those things I wanted to do that would make me feel like - like, I made it. But, it's not everything, and brand ambassador relationships should not be taken lightly. They are

2017 Flats & Handwashing challenge - the Flats Challenge is an annual event to call out diaper need and showcase how it could be supported using simple diapers and hand washing.

a lot of work and sometimes the relationship is not in favor of the content creator. I much enjoy creating content without the stress of appeasing a brand. I continued to build relationships with other brands - Nuggles Designs Canada, and my local retailer, CozyBums (closed).

In 2018, I started a podcast dedicated to cloth diapering - to branch out and try something that was considered to be the next 'it thing' for content creation. #allthebloggersweredoingit

On a family vacation to Eastern Canada, I visted the workshop for Mother-ease and dropped into the warehouse for Omaiki. Meeting the people behind these brands was incredible. They were everything I imagined. And reinstilled my need to get on the phone with brands for the podcast.

In October 2018, I accepted a position as the Director of Happiness at Nuggles Designs Canada. In this position, I write for Nuggles. I champion the brand on and offline. And I support her in creating an online community. Much has changed for Nuggles over the years, and I no longer create content for this brand as of 2020. This job would lead me to my other job, encourage me to study Public Relations, and become part of the catalyst towards content creation and the strategy of developing content/social media communities.

For many years, , I had a presumption I knew what I was doing and my way was the best way. I was toxic and held a lot of negative energy about brand expectations and general wash routine development. **But, one day, I had this AH HA moment...**

We all have our own story and experience with cloth diapering, wash routines, and products. This made cloth diapering grey - not black or white. Cloth diapering is a unique experience that lacks the peer-reviewed science for consistent results. Therefore, instead of insisting on rules for wash routines, we need to encourage and support people to make their own decisions that work for their family.

We also need to stop the judgement of brands based on rumour mills and start demanding transparency in their operations. This happens when they get in front of their story and tell it.

The Cloth Diaper Podcast is my project for telling these stories and unique experiences. I knew this could be an opportunity to chat to people in real life about why XYZ cloth diapering worked for them, or didn't. Because on the internet, people yell about how ABC is the only way to do things, but XYZ story is equally important.

I have had the great pleasure of talking with brands like Nerdy Mommas, Charlie Banana, Bambino Mio, Geffen Baby, s, and many other creators both big and small. It's been incredible learning their stories, challenges, and reflecting on how we can do better in this industry. I love being involved in this and I can't wait for more creators to continue to serve.

The Cloth Diaper Podcast still thrives and you can find me on Instagram, and content on YouTube. I don't create videos anymore

Visit www.clothdiaperpodcast.com to learn how to order a Cloth Diaper Mom shirt. May not be available. This is my design.

because I don't love video content. I'm a writer. Sometimes it's more fun to stay with the communication method that speaks to you. I do have dreams of establishing a video course to compliment that book, but give me time. The pandemic has thrown me for a curve ball. This book - this is where I am meant to be.

In 2019 I had two bunion surgeries. This meant I recorded episodes in bed with my cast. It was amazing to connect with online friends like this.

My cloth diapering journey and wash routine (you can find a video on my YouTube channel) is standard. I don't have finicky water or washing machines.. **But, it's not the only way to cloth diaper.** I want you to know there isn't one recipe to cloth diapering success. Don't get caught up in following the rules, being perfect, or never having a cloth problem.

Back to me - I'm not good at wash routine advice... I struggle with finding the answer for people and thats why I want to help you find the answer for you and be able to be indepdent in your cloth diaper experience. Yes, finding peers is important, but also knowing enough to troubleshoot yourself is empowering.

I love blogging and encouraging you to find your own answers. I love talking about brands, manufacturing, and the different styles of cloth diapers. I love the innovation of cloth dipaer brands. I love how brands can step up and make real change in this community. I love the cloth diaper community.

This book is my heart and soul - and everything I want you to know about cloth diapering.

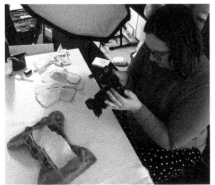

I tried to keep this simple and basic. This is a start here book. If you need more indepth information search my website or YouTube account, or message me on Instagram.

In my make shift photography studio creating IG content.

I'd love if you could leave a review of this book, wherever you purchased it and welcome you to connect with me online - @clothdiaperpodcast.

For more information and videos - www.clothdiaperpodcast.com.
Also, www.simplymombailey.com has most of my reviews and flats & handwashing content.

THIS IS THE BEGINNING OF ANYTHING YOU WANT.

QUICK START

Can I tell you everything you need to cloth diaper in one page?
No.

Cloth diapering is what you make it. With the onset of disposable diapering, we have to learn cloth diaper again. That's scary, but we can do it.

Cloth diapering is different than the stories of our grandparents. Diaper pins and flats are still in style, but cloth diapers have modernized and you have more options than ever.

To get started cloth diapering take a moment to consider:

1. **Why are you cloth diapering?**

   What are your motives? What do you want to achieve?

2. **What is your budget?**

   How much would you spend on disposable diapers? Cloth cost $10-40 each and you need 7-10 diaper changes per day. An average stash can cost upwards of $400, with high end stashes costing $700, and budget under $200

3. **What are your limitations?**

   Are there things that will make this hard? Daycare? Laundry facilities? Budget?

Many families start with enough diapers for a day. They wash & dry these 6-10 diapers every night. This is a low cost, low risk, entry to cloth diapering. **If you fall in love with cloth diapering, you can buy more cloth diapers**. If you hate a style of diaper that week, then you can try another. If you hate it all together, then you can move on. If you learn you need a weeks worth, then you can prioritize that budget and make it happen.

Choosing which diaper is best for you is the most overwhelming stage of the cloth diaper process. There is no right or wrong answer. **There is no best diaper.** Every diaper is amazing to someone.

Start with the diaper your friend recommends, or the prettiest diaper in the store, or the brand that captivates your heart. Put all the names in a hat and draw one. You really won't know which diaper will be best for you until you try.

But you can do this, you just need to start somewhere.

> Cloth diapering is simple.
> This is my decision.
> I can cloth diaper.

Keep these mantras present.

You can also download cloth diaper mantra's from www.clothdiaperpodcast.com
There will be moments where you feel **overwhelmed**.

There are moments where *cloth diapering feels really hard*.
There are going to be people who say you can't do it.
You can cloth diaper, and you will.
It's going to be okay.

The first step to cloth diapering is mindset.
Clear the lingering thoughts from the people who told you that you can't or you shouldn't or it's stupid or gross. They have one limited perspective of cloth diapering. These experiences do not have to be your story.

Recognize that **you are a bad ass.**
You can cloth diaper.
You can parent.
You can be you.

Your cloth diapering journey and mine are different. We are different people with different needs and priorities. That is okay.

This book has a lot of information in it, and you feel overwhelmed, that's okay. Let that feeling sink in. Motherhood is overwhelming.

YOU ARE CAPABLE OF AMAZING THINGS.

My Recommendations

1. Connect with cloth parents

Real stories and experiences are invaluable to your journey. Cloth diapering parents are wise. They offer support you need not only in cloth diapering but in motherhood. Trust in their recommendations, but follow your own instincts.

Other parents will offer advice that doesn't jive. This is okay. We learn as much from the conversation we disagree with as the ones we agree with. Take their thoughts, and your thoughts, and smash them together to come up with a solution that works.

2. Trust in cloth diaper brands & retailers

Wondering how to use your product?
Not sure if you can toss it in the dryer or if your water is too hot?
Check with a brand or retailer for product specific advice.
They know their product and they made it for you to succeed at cloth diapering. Let them help you

Cloth Diaper brand owners and retailers have years of wisdom in troubleshooting cloth diaper scenarios. They have been bombarded with random questions for years and might know easy answers to your predicament.

How do I find a retailer or local parents?
Ask. Some people don't flaunt it and you might find yourself pointed in the direction of a local Facebook community, local cloth diaper retailer or maybe someone in a bathroom stall at Walmart.

Or find a blogger like me - we have lists of our favourite shops and can point you in the right direction - clothdiaperpodcast.com/shop-cloth

3. March to the beat of your own rhythm

If we follow the song and dance of everyone else, we might find our-
selves klutzy and stumbling. March to the beat of your own rhythm
helps you find the routine, rhythm and moves needed to rock cloth
diapering.

You don't need fancy detergent if you don't want it.
You don't need cloth diaper accessories, or matching leggings.
They don't need to be the 'it' brand name, or new diapers.
You don't have to cloth diaper full time.
You can use disposables.

THIS IS YOUR JOURNEY AND IT MIGHT LOOK DIFFERENT THAN MINE, AND THAT'S OKAY.

*2015 - Folding cloth diaper
laundry with a newborn. This
is an angel folded prefold and
those are stacks of everything and
anything.*

*It's okay if you live out of the
hamper, or the machine. It's okay
if you fold your diapers and put
them away.*

**Find shortcuts that make
you happy.**

4. Don't place microfibre against the skin

Microfibre inserts do not go directly against the skin. Microfibre will over dry the skin and may cause irritation, rashes, and upset babies. *Some Microfibre inserts are wrapped in fleece or other textiles. This is okay to be against the skin because the microfibre material is covered.*

Microfibre is a synthetic material sought after because it's low-cost and efficient at absorbing liquid. It is commonly sold with pocket cloth diapers and feels itchy on the skin. Microfibre is defined by polyester terry loops.

5. Learn about natural fibres

Synthetics are cheap - microfibre, microfleece, microseude. It is a fibre derived from a petroleum base product. The best wash results for synthetics is to use hot water and syntehtic detergent. Synthetics like to hold to stink.

Natural fibres can be more expensive - cotton, hemp, and maybe bamboo. These fibres are derived from a plant source. Natural fibres are more forgiving to clean and more likely to work with natural detergents, cooler water, simpler routines can be effective.

Want to cloth diaper and use eco-friendly detergents?
Skip the synthetic textiles for a better cloth diaper experience.

6. Don't buy an entire stash of one type

It's easy to order two dozen pocket diapers and jump into cloth diapering. Consider one other style/brand/something when building a stash.

It's easier to have half a stash of diapers you don't like versus an entire stash of diapers that makes you want to quit. If an all-in-one diaper is the best choice - then try two different brands. If you're torn between two different types of diapers, then order half a stash in each and see which you like.

You don't know until you try.

If you want to cloth diaper at night, you might need something a little different like a thicker prefold, a fitted diaper, or something designed for heavy wetters. 8 hours versus 2 hours of daytime use.

7. Don't bank on resale $$$

You will read blogs or meet parents selling their stash for lots of money. It can be easy to get caught up in the game of - "I'll earn my money back" - but I caution you on this thinking. For many parts of the world, the cloth resale market is over saturated and may be difficult to sell your diapers.

Yes, you can sell your diapers, but don't get caught up that you will make your money back. Conservatively, you could get 25-50% back of the original price after 2-3 years of use.

On a good day, used diapers fetch 50% retail, but most go 25-40% of the original price. Some brands are highly sought after (HSA or HTF) and might go for the same price as retail. This can change at any moment. Brands are in flux and drama, new print, or a new brand can cause things to change by the time your done diapering.

During the time it took me to write this book, I watched one cloth diaper brand go from above retail prices on used to people struggling to give them away. This happens when a brand makes a call that impacts their social license to operate - also known as a crisis of reputation.

Cloth Diapering is not an investment.

STEPS TO CLOTH DIAPER

BUY THE DIAPERS

New from stores or brands, or used from other parents.

WASH THE DIAPERS

New diapers are prepped & used diapers are sanitized.

ASSEMBLE THE DIAPERS

Pair inserts with diapers, stuff pockets, fold in diapers

PUT IT ON BABY

The back of the diaper is the widest part, but the bum there and pass it through the legs. Use fasteners to fasten onto baby.

CHANGE BABY

When baby poops, or pees, or after 2 hours, change the diaper.

REPEAT TILL WASH DAY

Continue to put diapers on baby and change baby until wash.

ASSEMBLE THE DIAPERS

Pair inserts with diapers, stuff pockets, fold in diapers

WASH DIRTY DIAPERS

Use a simple wash routine as outlined by your brand or retailer to wash diapers.

AND REPEAT FOREVER.

PARTS OF A DIAPER

Before we even talk about the types

Cloth diapering is it's own language.
There is a glossary at the back with quick definitions for many of the common acronyms and words used in the cloth diaper space.

Different terms may be used in different parts of the world or within different communities. For example, in the UK they refer to snaps as poppers.

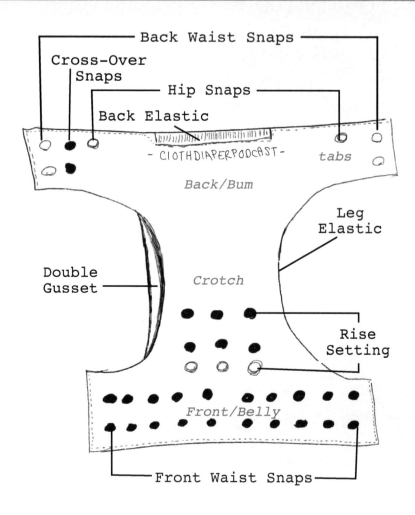

Cloth Diaper Sizing

The one size diaper (OS) is the most available cloth diaper on the market. The OS diaper is marketed for kids 8-35lbs (sometimes 10-40lbs), or birth to potty training. **One size diapers fit most kids.** There is always an exception. Some kids are small and some kids are big.

This is an example of a cheapie newborn diaper, One Size Lil Helper, and Plus Size Nerdy Mommas

This is an example of four one size cloth diapers. There is a lot of variation in this pile between the length and width. Some of that is because each diaper has a different rise and fit, but some of that is the variation of a one size diaper.

Rumparooz, bumGenius, Lil Helper and Bebeboo

Sized cloth diapers (as in size small, medium, and large) were popular around the turn of the century, but still available from limited providers. A common diaper to find in this kind of set up is FuzziBunz or Mother-ease Diapers. Purchasing sized diapers is cost prohibitive for many families. Sized diapers do offer a custom fit for babes at a specific size.

This is the Thirsties sized cover system. It's also available in a size 3. The prefolds and inserts come sized as well and gives you a full size run.

A popular sized option is the Size 1 & Size 2 system. This is a hybrid of traditional sized diapers and the one size system. We see this often with cloth diaper covers and fitted diapers as is popular with Esembly Baby, Bambino Mio, Thirsties, and many others.

Sometimes these diapers have rise settings and offer a better fit range for small or big babies. But sometimes not (as is shown on the Bambino Mio on the next page).

For example a size 1 diaper will fit 6-15lbs and a Size 2 will fit 15-40lbs. Many brands also produce sizes beyond this for preschoolers and big kids offering sizes 3 and 4 such as Thirsties, Best Bottom, and Petite Crown.

Size 1 & 2 systems allow for a more complete sizing range. Size 1 diapers are small for newborns and infants. Size 2 for babies and toddlers. This can be a great way to diaper newborns and big toddlers. It does have an extra cost but your stash may live longer through more kids and adapt to different life stages better.

A sized system is alos a better choice for fitted diapers because it gives you a better overall fit without excess bulk. This is seen in the Esembly Baby system and with Mother-ease. There are likely more brands too with awesome sized features.

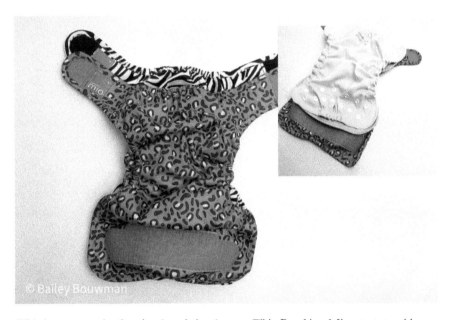

This is an example of a size 1 and size 1 cover. This Bambino Mio set up provides users with extended size flexibilty. Like everything, sizing is not standard. The size 1 Bambino Mio is much larger than other size one products such as the AppleCheeks Size 1

The newborn diaper is a sized diaper designed for babies 5-12lbs featuring newborn features and a trimmer fit. There is a limited supply of premie diapers and cloth diapers for smaller babies. These products are often found through WAHM or niche speciality shops on Etsy.

Looking for cloth diapers for larger kids and adults?

Yes, they exist. Many brands have larger diapers for kids 35 pounds plus aimed at bed-wetting preschoolers, or 40lb + kids. These diapers are sold as sized and one size variations under the names super, bigger, plus, or size 3 and usually sold direct from the brand.

This is a market that is in constant flux. Sometimes these diapers are available for short periods of time, sometimes the brand discontinues, sometimes something happens. It can be hard to find them.

The sunflower diaper from Bebeboo is an example of a One Size Diaper. The green diaper in the middle is from Snap-Ez and is a toddler/preschooler sized diaper and the bottom black one is a plus size pocket from Nerdy Momma to illustrate the size options.

The exterior of most cloth diapers is made of a waterproof material - PUL.

Some exceptions apply with fitted diapers and wool diapers, but PUL is the waterproof material on the exterior of most cloth diapers. It is a soft cotton (or poly/cotton) textile with a coating on one side that may or may not be visible to you. The coating is a chemical application heat bonded to the textile. PUL may feel smooth and plastic-like. It makes the diaper waterproof, but is still breathable.

PUL is found on most cloth diaper covers, pocket diapers and all in one diapers. PUL is sometimes added to training pants and used with swim diapers. PUL is a synthetic processed materials.

All TPU is PUL, but not all PUL is TPU.

Parents who say they prefer TPU often refer to the soft buttery and slightly stretchy variation of PUL material. Not all TPU feels like that and composition depends on the treatment applied.

PUL is short for polyurethane. PUL is the umbrella term for a treatment process of a laminate onto fabric. There are two processes: chemical or thermal. Chemical processing has largely faded in the past years. **TPU is short for thermal polyurethane.** This is a thermal process, or heat bond, of chemical that adds the waterproof barrier.

Laminate coatings differ between brands and is a closely guarded trade secret for many manufacturers - but much of it is made in a few factories in the USA and in China. There is a significant difference in cheap and expensive PUL/TPU products as the weight of the application varies.

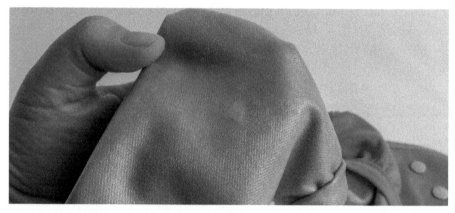

The above is broken PUL that is separating from the diaper after several years of use. You can see the shiney part (PUL application) and the matte part (fabric). This diaper gets wet spots on the exterior.

Most PUL has a wear life of 300-500 washes before it could start to break down. This depends on the quality of the material and application. PUL may break down quicker if exposed to high heats or caustic additives (like those in synthetic detergents, or bleach products).

Faulty PUL is known to delaminate within the first washes. The waterproof coating separating and bubbling from the original textile. Most brands should quickly recall and warranty any problems that arise. Email and/or call to discuss problems

PUL can't be repaired easily.

Frequently Asked Questions About PUL

Q: My PUL is leaking around the seams or stitching?
When a needle punches through the PUL it creates holes and sometimes (not often) they leak. These often seal up when tossed in the dryer on high heat for 15 minutes. Check with retailer or brand for specific advice. This is the most common recommendation. It might not work, and seam leaks can also be related to compression, poor absorption, or over-saturation.

Q: Can I wash PUL in hot water? Or the Sanitize Cycle?
Check with your brand for recommendations. PUL was initially developed to work in hospital enclaves but the product used with cloth diapers today is different and made for diapers not hospitals. Most PUL can handle hot water (max 140F) but brands have water temperature recommendations to ensure product longevity of the product, including washing shells in cold.

Q: Can I put PUL in the dryer?
Yes, most PUL can handle low to medium heat in the dryer. Again, brands will have ideal recommendations for longevity of their product. PUL dries really quickly. You can hang a cover to dry in a few hours.

Q: My PUL is wet!
Yes, sometimes a soaking wet insert pressed against perfectly good PUL will get wet. It's waterproof under good conditions but if you sit on it for a few hours a single layer PUL will leak. If the exterior textile gets wet, it will spreads across the rest of the cotton exterior of the diaper.

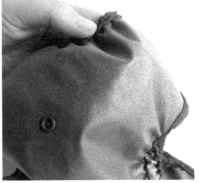

Q: There are scratches on the interior of the PUL?
Sometimes that happens from wash additives or elves or sharp spots in the machine. Unless it's causing leaks and wetness, it's usually okay and will work under normal conditions. Disclose when selling.

Absorbency, known as the inserts.

Cloth diapers need absorbent material to work. Where a disposable diaper has SAP gel in the mid section to absorb pee, cloth diapers use fabric or textiles to absorb liquid. This is the diapers *insert*. But I prefer the term **absorbency** because it's more inclusive of the options available including sewn in portions in diapers, prefolds and flats. An insert is a small rectangular pad sewn together.

Common textiles used in cloth diaper absorbency include: cotton, bamboo, hemp, and Microfibre.

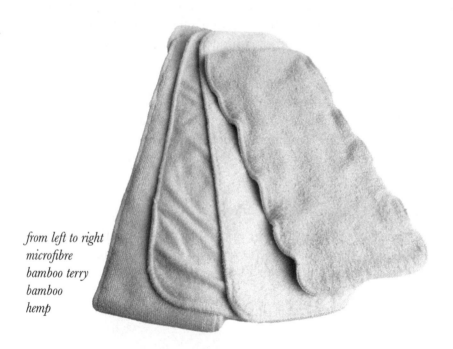

*from left to right
microfibre
bamboo terry
bamboo
hemp*

Textiles are blended with other textiles for optimal performance. They also come in different forms like gauze, jersey, and terry. The absorbency of an insert depends on the quality, weight and design of the insert, and not so much on the material.

Each textile has advantages. Fibre composition is not a sole indicator of product absorption. A cotton prefold will outperform a hemp booster, a bamboo fitted will outperform a hemp fitted. Absorbency is not just creating a list of textiles, but rather carefully considering the quality and design of a specific product. Talk to any up and coming brand and they will tell you their love of cloth diapers has now morphed into a fascination with textiles.

Cotton, bamboo, and hemp are natural fibres and can go directly against the skin. Microfibre, fleece, micro-fleece, micro-suede and some athletic wicking jerseys are synthetic fibres. Microfibre is the only one that cannot touch the skin for long periods of time

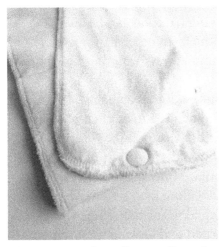

To the left is the Smart Bottoms Cotton Insert. The top is the Thirsties Cotton insert; two product examples for cloth diapering products.

Cotton

Cotton is a cheap natural fibre manufactured around the world. Cotton farms in the United States provide local cotton to many American mills that are then used in manufacturing of cloth diapers. But many brands source cotton through international channels.

Cotton is considered to be an energy intensive textile crop using many pesticides, herbicides, water, and resources to grow. Organic cotton provides an alternative that attempts to reduce the impacts of the cotton industry.

Cotton for cloth diapers is often an organic product with certifications. These certifications can always be verified with the brands, with most brands sharing proof upon request. Not all cotton for cloth diapers is organic.

Cotton is available in bleached and unbleached forms. This implies cotton has undergone a bleaching process to whiten the fibres. This results in fewer oils in the products for easier , but not always. Cotton fibres will whiten with time, but do easily stain.

Cotton is sold as a knit material or birds-eye material. It is found in flats, prefolds and All In One Diapers diapers. Cotton inserts and boosters are less common. Cotton can be sold as 100% cotton product, but is blended with other textiles, like hemp, to create exciting cloth products.

Cotton is cheap, absorbent, and easy to clean. Cotton textiles dry quickly (unless a dense pile of 6+ layers). Depending on the density and weight of the material, cotton can be prone to compression when fully saturated, but less compression than microfibre. Cotton is one of the easiest textiles to re-purpose. You can take any cotton product and use it as a cloth diaper insert or absorbency.

Bamboo

Bamboo is a cheap processed natural fibre. Bamboo agriculture and manufacturing happens in Asia. Growing bamboo can be a very sustainable process, but like anything the farming of bamboo can be abused resulting in deforestation. Bamboo grows very quickly without the use of pesticides.

Milling bamboo from a stalk into a fibre is a chemical process requiring carbon disulfide. Carbon disulfide is a toxic chemical when mishandled. Not all bamboo milling is done responsibly - increasing concerns around this process happens at mills in countries outside of China, including Indonesia and India. Many cloth diaper companies opt to purchase bamboo milled in a close loop system where the chemicals are recycled instead of dumped post-processing. Always ask the retailer or brand if you are concerned and looking for additional information.

The chemical processing of bamboo creates a rayon material that is spun into a textile. Bamboo is fairly synthetic at this stage. It's been heavily processed. Tencil or Lyocell is a different processing

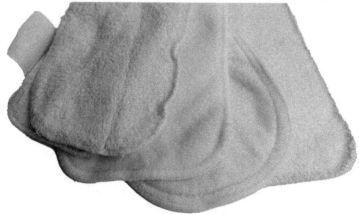

Various types of Bamboo inserts including Nuggles, Wink Diapers, Funky Fluff, and Peachy Baby. Notice the slightly yellowing colour of the textile and the variation in the pile of the textile. Many different weaves, densities and variations.

method using different, or less chemicals. These materials are not common in mainstream cloth diapering at the writing of this book, but available through work-at-home creators.

Bamboo is sold as a knit, jersey, or terry cloth. It is found in inserts or prefolds. Bamboo is almost always blended with cotton, sometimes hemp. Bamboo blends are 70% bamboo and 30% cotton. Knit variations of bamboo are likely to shrink overtime, while terry cloth holds it shape.

Bamboo is versatile in that different blends, weights, and products perform differently. Generally, is quick to absorb, but may be prone to compression at fully saturation with less-dense products.

Hemp

Hemp is a natural fibre. It is renowned for having a short growth cycle, minimal water requirements, doesn't need any herbicides or pesticides, and gives back to the soil. Unfortunately, the stigma around hemp delays and limits development, sale and availability.

Hemp is considered a low environmental impact textiles when considering the agricultural and milling processes.

Hemp is sold as a blended product; typically, blended with cotton for a ratio of 40% hemp and 60% cotton. Geffen Baby manufactures the highest hemp ratio with a 60% hemp blend insert. Check

Hemp is typically sold as a 2-3 layer insert like shown above - HempBabies, AMP Diapers, Geffen Baby, and random Cheapie.

out the Cloth Diaper Podcast to read an interview with the owner of Geffen Baby about their product and process. Hemp knit products or sometimes a fleece-like textile, and sold as a booster or insert.

Hemp is sought after for it's absorbing capacity. Considered one of the highest absorbers on the market, the overall performance of hemp is up for debate. Hemp is a slow absorber with very little compression. A 100% hemp product would be impractical for use, and thus blends give improved product performance. *Buy hemp not because it's absorbent but because of it's performance - ability to hold liquids and reduce compression.*

Hemp is an expensive textile. There are noticeable differences between cheap and expensive hemp that includes absorption rates, laundering performance, and overall product durability. Cheaper hemp is more yellow and prone to shriveling like bacon. Cheaper hemp products are also slower to dry. More expensive hemp products give better performance.

Microfibre

Microfibre is a synthetic fibre used because of absorbing capabilities and low-cost point. Microfibre can hold 7-8 times weight in liquid, but it is prone to compression (when you squeeze a product - even lightly - and water leaks out).

Microfibre is spun from polyester. Polyester is made from

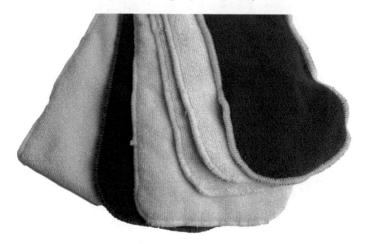

Different types of microfibre Blueberry Diapers, Coffee Microfibre, Imagine Baby, Cheapie, and Lil Helper Charocoal Bamboo Microfleece.

petrochemicals. Overtime microfibre sheds. Textile shedding happens with all products including cotton, bamboo and hemp. With microfibre it breaks down is a synthetic plastic particle contributing to overall concerns around micro-plastic pollution in our waterways, specifically oceans.

This shedding of microfibre impacts product longevity. Microfibre can become flat after 2-3 years use. Microfibre is difficult to clean. You might use microfibre in your home already to clean things and know it does a fantastic job of holding onto dirt and grime; for that reason, microfibre can be difficult to clean requiring hot water, synthetic detergents, and maybe the occasional bleach wash (as per manufacturers instructions).

Microfibre is sold as an insert - 2-4 layers. Microfibre is sewn into many All In One diapers, and sometimes added to other inserts to create combinations, including wrapped in fleece. Pair microfibre with natural fibres for improved performance including wrapping in a cotton flat, or adding hemp under it.

This is an example of wrapping microfibre in an Osocozy cotton flat. This is a great strategy for an overnight diaper.

Cloth Diaper Insert Absorbency Chart

www.clothdiaperpodcast.com

Microfibre	Cotton	Bamboo	Hemp
$ Cheapest	$ Cheap	$$ Costly	$$$ Expensive
Synthetic	Natural Fibre	Processed Fibre	Natural Fibre
100% microfibre, sometimes wrapped in fleece	100% cotton or blends with bamboo/hemp	70% Bamboo and blended with cotton or hemp.	40-50% hemp and blended with bamboo or cotton
Breaks down with time (~2 year)	Edgewear happens on inserts	Knits shrinks & terry becomes less fluffy	Cheaper variations prone to shrinkage and twisting
Quick Absorber	Okay Absorber	Quick Absorber	Slow Absorber
Prone to Compression	Compression can occur	Depends on the blend	Not likely to compress

Absorbency depends on product quality, density, and blend.

Anything can be an insert

If it absorbs liquid - it is an insert. It is that simple.
You can re-purpose any cotton or bamboo textiles in your home for
your diaper. Try to find things with 90%+ natural fibre.

Don't get caught up in the terminology.
Absorbent materials are interchangeable. Natural fibre inserts can be
put in covers, flats in pockets, and boosters added to any cloth diaper.

Micro-fleece, micro-suede, fleece, silk, and athletic wicking jersey are
common stay dry materials and liners found in cloth diapers. These
materials are not significantly absorbent.

*A womens XL T-shirt cut in half and folded into a pad to fit into a Nuggles pocket diaper
for an insert. T-shirts are great way to repurpose a product around your home without
added cost. T-shirt absorbency varies depending on size, but a full sized large shirt works
overnight for many kids.*

Frequently Asked Questions about Absorbency

Q: What textile is the best for absorbency?
The one that works for your child.
Different kids pee differently and many families find hemp too slow, or cotton not absorbent enough, or bamboo inefficient. Start somewhere. Cotton and bamboo are great for general absorbency, and hemp is awesome for boosters.

Q: What is the most absorbent product for heavy wetters?
It's important to acknowledge what you have tried first, and finding a scale of where you sit. There are absorbency lists on the Internet including my own website and All About Cloth Diapers. Compare the products you have tried and find a product more absorbent. This might be a bamboo prefold or a fitted diaper, or just a booster.

Q: Is Microfibre an okay product?
Yes, Microfibre is okay to use. It is standard in cloth diapers as an insert because it's cheap and absorbent. Compression, synthetic nature, and bulkiness can be discouraging to some people. If you want to use natural detergents, microfibre might not be a good fit.

Q: Can I mix and match textiles?
Yes, you can. It might take some experimenting to find a combo that works for you as you judge your child's flow, and compression needs.

Q: What about charcoal bamboo? or coffee Microfibre?
 There is little evidence that charcoal or coffee additions can reduce smells, heal skin, or other health claims. These additions primarily change the colour of the textile. This is more frequently being done on entry level cloth diapers to reduce staining and discolouration

Q: Can my child be allergic to a textile?
Some children react to textiles when used as a cloth diaper. You can have a perfect routine but swapping to other textile fibres makes a difference. We have heard stories of children reacting to bamboo, and only using cotton - and vice versa. Sometimes it's not the detergent, its the material.

Interior lining of a diaper.

Different textiles line the interior of a diaper. The exterior is PUL and the interior is either exposed PUL or a textile lining. This material is usually stay dry and not absorbency.

- For pocket cloth diapers: the lining creates the pocket of the diaper with an opening allowing you to add inserts. If you turn the pocket inside out you will find the PUL layer.

- For an All In One diapers, and some covers, liners protect the PUL or add a stay-dry experience to the body of the diaper.

Common liners are made of stay dry material such as micro-fleece, regular fleece, microseude, or athletic wicking jersey. Some diapers have liners made of cotton or bamboo. These are not stay dry diapers. Some diapers use a second layer of PUL to line the diaper for extra wetness protection.

This is an example of the interior lining on an Omaiki All In One diaper that used athletic wicking jersey.

37

Frequently Asked Questions about the Lining

Q: Water just beads up on top of the liner?

This is typical of synthetics linings because it needs compression from the body to encourage the liquid to pass through to the insert. If there is a layer of scum, then you have build up, but otherwise it's an inconvenient reality.

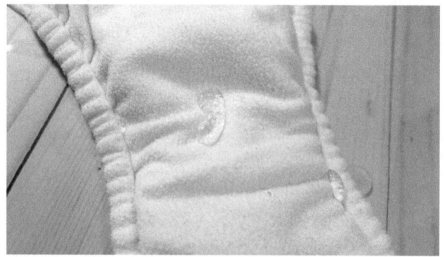

If you just pour water on any fleece diaper, like this Charlie Banana, beading happens, its because fleece kinda sucks, and the weight of the body will help.

Q: Will my baby get hot with fleece diapers?

There is no research based evidence at this time suggesting cloth diapers are warmer or cooler than disposable diapers.

Many people perform experiments at home and show evidence that may suggest cloth is cooler. Some companies rely on athletic wicking jersey as a cooler textile than fleece.

Q: Can I get natural fibre pocket diapers?

Most pocket lining are synthetic. There are very few natural-fibre options. People like the easy-clean up of a pocket, but the stay-dry continues to be popular.

Q: My baby gets a moisture rash, will stay dry diaper help?

No guarantees a stay-dry lined diapers help with rashes anymore than any other textile. Change baby regularly and pat dry between changes.

Q: What about grey coloured fleece liners?

A trend in 2021 is that brands are now creating coloured inners - usually grey suede material. This is to reduce the appearance of staining. Staining is cosmetic, but it does bother many families. Grey inners can be a great choice to keep diapers looking fresh. Available in seude and micro fleece.

This is an example of a grey inner on a Cutie Patootie All In Two Diaper, the white on a La Petite Ourse Pocket, and a coloured fleece on the Imagine Baby. Please note that the internral gusset designs on these pocket diapers is only available in Canada.

Q: What is the best stay-dry material?

I am impartial to athletic wicking jersey because it cleans up nicely and less heavy than fleece. But, fleece and suede are more common.

Q: Can I reuse a lined cover?

Yes. While, many say no, as long as the cover remains clean, then it can be reused. If it becomes soiled or stinky, then stop reusing. If this disgusts you, then don't do it.

Leg \ of a diaper.

Yes, the leg elastic in cloth diapers are not all the same. Brands and styles approach elastics differently.

Apple Cheeks Ruffles.
Best Bottom Gusset design.
Lil Helper Encased Elastic.

Encased elastics is a standard elastic casing. A tube is made by folding the PUL onto itself along the edge of the diaper. The elastic is threaded through and sewn in at both ends. This simple encased elastic is common on many diapers, and one of the easiest to replace depending on how it was sewn into the diaper.

Ruffled elastic diapers have sewn in elastics. Elastics are directly sewn into the diaper, and a ruffle on the exterior with serged PUL. This is a gentle fit some people love or struggle with.

Fold over elastic is a wide elastic that is folded over the edge of the diaper and sewn in place. Fold over elastic (FOE) is common in made at home diapers as because it's available in DIY kits.

This is an example of how a rolled elastic fits on an All In One diaper, such as the Blueberry Simplex.

Rolled elastics is an elastics sewed in and rolled. I don't really know how to describe how this is done. The elastic seam is one side absorbent material and one side PUL and found in all-in-one diapers. The absorbent material may roll out and needs to be rolled back towards the centre to prevent leaking. Absorbent material on the exterior of the diaper will cause leaks.

Double gusset diaper is an additional sewn in panel in the leg of the diaper with a second row of leg elastics. A gusset is a piece of material sewn into a garment to enlargen the material, and in the cloth diaper community this is referred to as a double gusset as there is one on each side of the diaper to give the diaper more girth.

In most diapers, the interior elastic on the added material is placed in the crease of the leg.

This is an example of a double gusset on a cover from Bebeboo Diapers.

Interior gusset is an elastic sewn into the lining of the diaper creating a channel in the body of the diaper.

This is a patent design held by KangaCare in the USA to create a channel for body fluids. You will find this style of gusset outside of the USA on other brands.

Frequently Asked Questions about Elastics

Q: Does my diaper need a gusset to prevent leaks?
No. Gussets don't solve all problems. Diapers without gussets are designed to work without them. For example, the Flip diaper is a wide crotch to fit inserts, but can still be trim between the legs. Well-designed cloth diapers without gussets provide leak-proof experiences.

If you want to fit a thick stack of inserts into a cloth diaper then a double gusset be the right choice for you. Or a diaper wide enough to handle it.

Q: Why do my leg elastics sag and not fit close baby.
Two reasons jump to mind, the first is your elastics are too long. To adjust the elastics adjust the rise setting of the diaper to make it shorter to fit the baby. Elastics sometimes are stretched out after years of use and then need to be replaced. If you need tighter leg elastics but your leg elastics are stretched out, try pulling the top corner of the waist panel up and over the diaper to create a bunny ear like look.

The second is that your inserts are too big or bulky. Inserts need to fit your child and long inserts or thick inserts will push the diaper away from the body and the elastics too.

Q: How do I replace leg elastics?
If elastics go, some can be replaced. The ones in tubes are most easy to replace while sewn in elastics are more challenging. There are tutorials online for each diaper type as well as people who will replace elastics. Local seamstresses charge $7-15 per diaper to replace elastics plus shipping. These fees may change depending on where you are.

I tried to replace the elastics on a GroVia AIO and ended up ripping out the seam and hand stitching it in place instead of just rethreading the elastic. This seam took me forever. Always think about your skills, do some reading and videos, before embarking on elastic repairs. It can be easy but it can be trouble.

Q: The material sticks out on my rolled elastics. How do I fix that?

Roll the elastic towards the inside of the diaper when folding them or before use. This can be done by pulling the absorbent inner into the mid section of the diaper. This tug rolls the elastic the other way allowing the absorbent material to fall inside the diaper instead of outside. If the diaper is already on your child and continues to roll out, push the textile material back into the diaper using your hands.

Recently, a seamstress informed me that a well constructed diaper should not roll out like this. What she meant is there are certain tricks sewers can use to adjust the pattern and ensure that this nuisance doesn't happen. Many diapers will roll inwards on their own.

My struggle with this on some diapers is not ideal. The diapers shown below are from Smart Bottoms, a well-respected cloth diaper in the industry that I struggle with rolled elastics. This may have been the result of that particular batch, or user error. Many times brands will change their products to reflect changing needs in teh community.

The absorbent inner on the black diaper sticking out - this is the struggle with rolled elastics. The top is much more tucked into the diaper.

Q: How do I protect my elastics?

Elastics are impacted by heat, UV Rays, urine, detergent and time. Avoid stretching hot diapers. Before storing diapers ensure diapers are thoroughly clean, of excess detergent and can breathe during storage.

Q: Do I need to hang my diapers a certain way?

There are many opinions about the way to hang diapers but little evidence to prove one way or the other is beneficial to the longevity of a diaper. In my experience, washing machine agitators destroy elastics, not short-term hanging experiences. If you feel the weight is impacting the elastics, then hang them to reduce that impact.

Q: My diapers guve my child red marks on her skin that don't go away.

If the marks go away, it's no big deal, but sometimes they don't. There can be a few reasons for this:

1) Urine build up in the elastics overnight cause a burn (try more absorbency so it doesn't flood to the elastics)
2) Detergent build up in the elastics (try using less detergent)
3) Elastics are too tight (adjust the fit and sizing of the diaper)
4) Elastic reactions (rare but some kids don't handle elastic rubbers)
5) Something else.

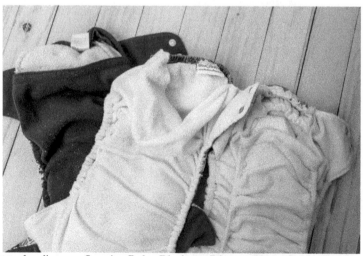

Different pocket diapers - Imagine Baby, Blueberry Diapers, KangaCare | Rumparooz

Exterior fasteners on a diaper

The exterior fasteners on the diaper adjust the size and shape to custom fit your baby. They are located on the wing of the diaper. These wings extend from the back and come in a variety of different shapes (image below).

Most cloth diapers fasten at the front, and a few at the side, using snaps or hook & loop. The ones at the top and bottom of the diaper are the waist snap of the diaper.

Over the years we have seen these fasteners change shape and get larger. Most common configuration is a double snap with some sort of hip snap.

This image shows the Kangacare | Rumparooz Pcoket Diaper amongst the bumGenius, Lil Helper and Bebeboo. The top, smaller cuts, are some of the original cloth diapers from the early 2000's. But most diapers being created today now feature a larger cut.

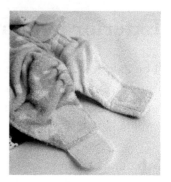

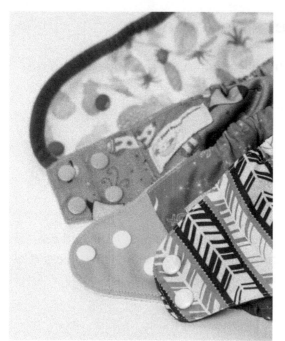

Hook & Loop tabs are an option for some brands giving ease of use fastening.

Popular hook & loop diapers include La Petite Ourse, Thirsties, GroVia, and Nicki's Diapers.

This is an example of different types of waist snaps found on cloth diapers - Thirsties, Sweet Peas, Nerdy Mommas, Imagine Baby

A fastener can be snaps or hook and loop. Snaps on the back wings of the diapers fasten to the snaps at the very front top of the diaper. There are many different combinations of snaps to fasten the diaper. Some diapers have two rows of snaps, some have a single row of snaps. Some diapers have hip snaps and some do not.

When finding the best fit on the waist snaps pull the wings across the front and fasten so the diaper fits snug along the belly. The material should not be strained or too loose. You should be able to fit your finger comfortably into the front of the diaper.

Frequently Asked Snap Questions

Q: Which snap do I snap first?
I don't think it matters; you will find your groove.
I like to snap the hip snaps first and then the waist snaps.

Q: Can my snaps be off centred?
Does the diaper fit your baby? Doesn't fall off or pinch the baby? Then you are good to go because it doesn't have to be perfectly symmetrical.

Q: What's the deal with cross over snaps?
Cross over snaps are the set of female snaps on the wing of the diaper. These are for the smallest of bellies allowing you to cross the wings onto each other if the baby is small.

You can use these to roll the diaper up into a little ball for your diaper bag when out and about.

Q: Do I need a hip snap? Or use it?
No. You do not need a hip snap, and you don't have to use it. Everything is optional.

Hip snaps are a nice-to-have instead of a must-have. If you notice **wing droop**, where the front panel of the diaper sags onto the leg, using the hip snap will prevent that sag.

You can also pull the front corners up and over the diaper to help tighten elastics. This will look like wings above the diaper.

Q: Which snap configuration is the best?
Personal preference. *I love a double waist snap over the triangle variations or the single snap. Many families prefer a single snap.*

Q: What if my snaps break?

Snaps can be replaced using a snap press.
Check the brand warranty. It may be replaced depending on warranty. Snaps are relatively easy to replace with the right tools.

Q: Are all snap sizes the same?

Mostly. Most cloth diaper brands use standard KAM snaps. GroVia is the most common exception in that they use a custom sized snap.

Other thoughts on waist fasteners.

Quality matters.
Cheaper diapers have fewer snaps, often with poor arrangements. This impacts the overall fit and function of the diaper. Options are good. 6 poorly spaced snaps can be a frustrating experience.

Hook & loop diapers are easier for hands that struggle with fastening snaps. Some brands use brand name Velcro or Aplix, while others use their own patent creations or generic product. Quality also matters for hook and loop fasteners. Knock-off hook and loop falls apart and breaks down. Yellowing is normal. Getting lint caught up in the hooks is normal. Clean it out using a pin or sharp pointy object. It takes patience. Oh, and use the laundry tabs!

Sometimes you'll find waist fasteners on the side!

Side snapping diapers, *like this variation from GroVia,* is a less common configure. But they exist. They give a snug fit with some learning curve. Check with the brand for resources on how to use this diaper style effectively for fit.

Rise snaps - those things in the middle.

One size cloth diapers (and some sized diapers) feature rise snaps in the mid front of the diaper underneath one or two rows of waist snaps. Rise snaps present in many combinations - 2-3 across and 2-5 options down.

The top snap is a male snap with an extending protrusion that snaps down to a lower rows to adjust the length of the diaper. This makes the diaper shorter or longer as the baby grows and changes.

2x3 rise setting

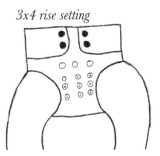

3x4 rise setting

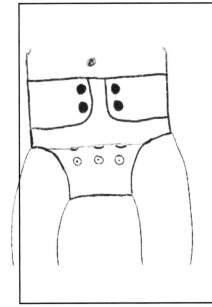

General sizing guidelines:

Smallest Setting: 8 to 12-15lbs
Second Setting: 15 - 25lbs
Open Setting: 25 lbs +

Weight guidelines provided are a suggestion. Your child's body shape influences the rise setting and you may find other adjustments give a better fit.

Frequently Asked Questions about Rise Settings

Q: When do I adjust the rise setting?

Adjust the rise setting if it is difficult to fasten the diaper onto the baby without pinching or if there are gaps in the legs, or bum crack showing, or other poor fit characteristics. If the rise snaps look pulled or tight, it might be time to open them or adjust the inserts to be less bulky/thick.

Adjust the rise setting to give your baby the best fit regardless of the weight recommendations. Many families open the diaper around 6-9 months, and then go down a rise setting again at 18 months. It's okay to have rise settings change through the year.

The size of the diaper changes with the rise setting from tiny to big. This is shown in the Baby Koala diapers shown above.

Q: Do unsnap rise settings for wash day?

No. Leave the rise snaps snapped and the diaper should wash up fine.

Q: Does the number of rise snaps matter?

Not really. It's a style thing. Three across gives a nice smooth front of diaper surface that is less likely to bulge. Four across is overkill.

The number of rows gives you options. Four rows of rise snaps allows for a smaller fitting diaper compared to a standard 3 rows.

Q: Where does the rise snap material go?

Most brands recommend pushing the fold up towards the belly button. This tightens the elastics and reduces leaking out of the leg crease/gap.

To do this, put your finger in the space between the snaps and push the fold up towards the belly button. This will leave a smooth crease along the mid-section of the diaper.

Not all diapers respond this way, some brands just need to be left to lay. This push up can be an aesthetic thing over function, but sometimes it is functional. It really depends on the cut of the diaper, the placement of the elastics and the location of the snaps. If you are experiencing leaks out of the legs of the diaper, it can be one area to play around with.

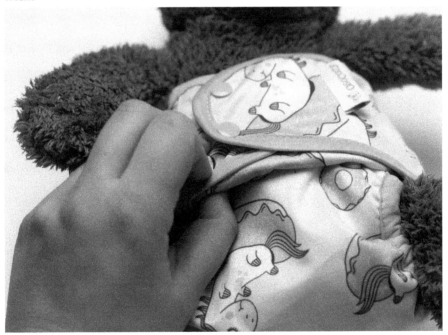

Simply push the material up. You should get a clean crisp line across the rise setting on this Osocozy Cover.

Diapers without rise snaps

There are a couple of reasons a cloth diaper might not have rise settings: sized diaper, internal rise settings, fold down rise, or newborn waist sizing.

Sized diapers do not have rise settings because the diaper fits for a specific weight range given. This is common on sized diapers, *such as Mother-ease and AppleCheeks diapers.*

Some one size diapers have internal settings to adjust the length of the diaper. This is done with the leg elastics. Toggles on the leg elastic adjust them to give a smaller or larger fit.

Quick April 2021 Update - The Charlie Banana patented toggle is now found on the Pampers Pure Hybrid Diaper. This style of toggle is highly inaccessible and difficult for families ot use.

The internal toggles on Charlie Banana and SoftBums featured below.

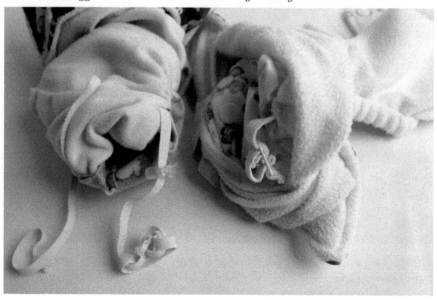

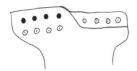

A fold down rise is found on fitted cloth diapers. To change the length of the diaper the front is folded down and a set of snaps is now visible to be used. These snaps are then used to adjust the waist.

You'll find a fold down rise on many fitted cloth diapers (work-at-home-mom) like the Lilly & Frank shown below, and demo'd on my young daughter on a brand no longer in production.

Newborn waist sizing - this is the rise setting used on many newborn cloth diapers and refers to two rows of waist snaps on the front of the diaper but only one snap on the wing of the diaper. Match the snap to a higher or lower setting depending on the thigh size. This is pictured below using the Imagine Baby newborn all in one diaper.

Internal panels and flaps.

There are different parts inside the diaper from flaps to extra PUL. You might be curious what they are, the purpose, and more. I'm always learning too. Check with brands to learn how to best use your diaper.

Examples of different panels on diapers. The Imagine Baby has no panel, the Nuggles Simplee has a small panel, and the Bebeboo has a belly panel.

A belly panel is a strip of PUL found inside the diaper towards the top-front (where the snaps are, but inside).
This strip of material reduces front wicking (moisture leaks along the edge of the diaper). Leaking at the front is common with boys, with compression from car seats or baby wearing, the use of diaper shirts/onsies, and some pants, particularly those that cut into the waist. It is common to place the insert under the panel to allow function as shown below with the La Petite Ourse Pocket (right).

Belly panels can be a big flap and sometimes half a strip. Sometimes on pockets they cover an opening like is shown on the Cutie Patootie Diaper (left).

The top diaper has no flap, but the bottom one does

Inside flaps are found on some diapers.

These flaps are made of PUL and found at the front and/or the back. Some flaps are designed to tuck the insert into and some are not. This tuck and go style diaper keeps the insert in place. Some flaps are just used as reinforcement of the snaps, or to add additional water resistance to the diaper.

Snaps on the inside of the diaper

Some diapers feature snaps on the inside. These might be found on the liner, or on the PUL. They are designed for inserts to snap into them. You don't have to use them, but if you want an insert to be held in place they are there to help you.

Diapers with internal snaps are sometimes marketed as an all in two or snap-in-diaper. They are sometimes mistakenly sold as an all in one diaper.

SOMETIMES,
THE ONLY WAY
TO STAY SANE
IS TO GO A
LITTLE CRAZY

TYPES OF DIAPERS

Now it's time to choose

Types of diapers

All In One - one piece diaper
All In Two or Snap In One - multi functional two piece diaper
Pocket Diapers - two piece diaper
Covers - exterior waterproof cover
Newborn - designed for newborns
Trainers - training underwear for potty training
Swim Diapers - designed for swimming
Fitted Diapers - absorbent diapers, not waterproof
Hybrid - blended styles

ALL IN ONE DIAPER
The diaper that is everything in one

Abbreviation: AIO

An All In One cloth diaper is a diaper with sewn in absorbency. This diaper is a **grab-and-go style** of diaper. It is most likely to be one piece, with maybe a detachable booster.

A piece of absorbent material is sewn into the diaper creating what looks like a "tongue." This tongue lays across the diaper or is folded into the diaper. Some AIO diapers have sewn in absorbency in the shell of the diaper or attached to either end).

General Assumptions

- More expensive.
- Typically natural fibres.
- Prone to wash-wear.
- Less likely to be a stay dry.
- Bulkier fit if Microfibre.
- One size or newborn.
- Lengthy dry time.
- More finicky to clean.
- Absorbency varies.
- Use booster or inserts to increase absorbency.

A few common styles of AIO diaper include diapers.
- Sewn in absorbency, completely or both ends.
- Tongues, long or short. Long ones are folded.
- Snap-in absorbency, boosters or main.

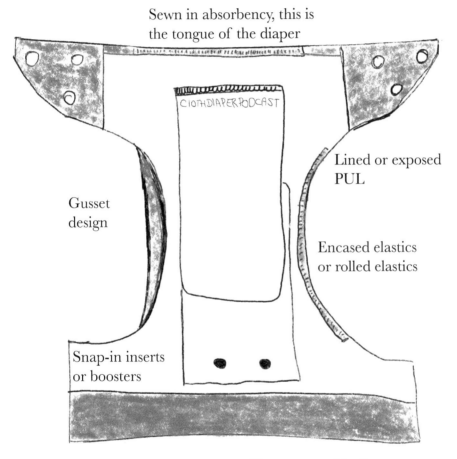

Sewn in absorbency, this is the tongue of the diaper

CLOTHDIAPERPODCAST

Lined or exposed PUL

Gusset design

Encased elastics or rolled elastics

Snap-in inserts or boosters

Tummy panel in front

Stack of All In One diapers featuring Omaiki, bumGenius, Thirsties and AppleCheeks. My daughter is featured in the Smart Bottoms AIO below.

Bailey's Favourite

I have had a mixed relationship with AIO diapers. I fell in love with the Blueberry Simplex but quickly got frustrated with stuffing the tongue of the diaper into the pocket and rolling the rolled elastics.

Currently, my favourite AIO is the Omaiki AIO, Mother-ease Uno, and bumGenius Elemental (no particular order). I like a natural fibre AIO with sewn in absorbency that does not require folding. In my experience, AIO diapers are excellent day-time diapers, but poorly performed at night for my heavy wetter child. They did work for my daughter so it's about the unique output needs of each child.

I always toss my AIO diapers in the dryer knowing that it breaks down the fibres quicker but keeps me sane longer. I'm okay with this risk. Sometimes best practice is not the best choice for my life. And I own the fact that these decisions can void my warranty.

I have **Best of Lists** available at www.clothdiaperpodcast.com to reflect new and upcoming cloth diaper brands.

Frequently Asked Questions about AIO Diapers

Q: Why are AIO diapers so expensive?
Because it's everything you need in one package - the absorbency to the waterproof cover. AIO diapers have increased material and labour costs associated with their production.

Cheaper AIO diapers use synthetics and manufacture overseas. AIO diapers start around $20 USD, or $30 CAD. A day of diapers (6 changes) will cost you upwards of $120 USD and a 3 day stash can be $600+. A low-cost AIO to consider is the La Petite Ourse AIO.

Q: Can I put AIO diapers in the dryer?
Yes, most brands will allow low to medium dryer use. Many AIO will dry in the dryer on medium in one cycle. The most dense part of the diaper will be the hardest to dry - sections where there are multiple layers of natural fibres.

If you live somewhere humid, air drying might be impractical.

Q: I air dry my AIO and they are stiff?
Natural fibres stiffen up when air dried, try shaking them, or toss them in the dryer on low with a tennis ball and they should soften up. Crunchy diapers will not hurt your child.

Q: Is this an AIO Diaper? It has snap-in inserts??
Some brands market an AIO cloth diaper with snap-in inserts instead of sewn in absorbency. Nobody legislates what is or isn't an AIO diaper. I find that this type of system unsnaps in the wash, but many not everyone has this experience. You will also find these diapers marketed as a snap in one diaper.

This is the Nicki's AIO Diaper. It's an example of how some diapers are labeled one thing and different than the standard definition.

Q: My AIO diapers have holes in them? Is that normal?

Yes, and no. Many natural fibres wear down with use. This is called edge wear. It's normal. Depending on the wash routine (detergent strength, agitation, water pH, and more factors) edge wear happens quicker for some people. This happens with fitteds too.

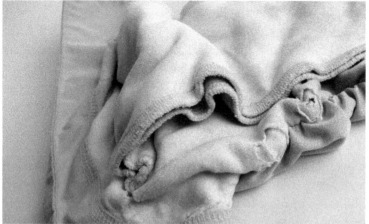

Edge wear in this original bumGenius Elemental AIO diaper appeared after 3 years of heavy use. The diaper functions great and can continue to be used.

Q: My AIO diaper isn't absorbent enough.

Sometimes that happens, and the best way to boost the absorbency is with small inserts known as boosters. You can use a folded up cloth wipe, or a specifically designed booster. For the best experience fold the booster or inserts in half and place it where your child wets most, the front for boys the mid-section for girls.

I've layered a Hemp Babies insert on top of an All In One diaper, just as is.

Q: Can I use an AIO overnight?

Maybe, depends on how much absorbency your child needs. Some AIO diapers hold over 10 ounces, others hold about 6 ounces. Not all AIO diapers are the same, but all can be boosted using inserts or prefolds. Try the Nerdy Mommas AIO or Diaper Rite AIO for nights.

Q: How do I make my AIO diaper stay dry?

Most AIO diapers are made of natural fibres and not stay dry. Use a micro-fleece liner made from fleece blankets, or purchased specifically for this. Place the liner in the interior of the diaper. This liner is only used once and gives a stay dry experience. You can also use silk liners or athletic wicking jersey liners.

Q: What about AIO with sewn in inserts...

Most AIO diapers have sewn in inserts, but it's usually just one side. I wanted to talk to you about AIO with sewn in inserts that are completly stitched in because you must be cautious if you want a good fit as shown in the images below. If the insert is too long it will not fit on small babies and stick out. Instead, look for well thought out products like the La Petite Ourse AIO or the Melissa Makes AIO that have it sewn in the middle to the back. This gives a better fit and reduces front leaks. The disadvantage to this type of AIO is longer dry times.

POCKET CLOTH DIAPER
The diaper everyone thinks they love

Abbreviation: none.

A pocket cloth diaper is a diaper with an exterior water-proof shell and an interior layer (typically stay dry). An opening between the two layers is found at the top or bottom and inserts are placed between the two layers.

General Assumptions

- One Size, or Bigger/Plus.
- Stay dry (various textiles).
- Back pocket or front pocket.
- Sold with Microfibre inserts.
- Bulk depends on absorbency used.
- Easy(er) poop clean up.
- Single leg elastic, gussets in some brands.
- Cheaper system when purchased with Microfibre.
- Two step diaper - absorbent material needs to be "stuffed" inside.
- May need to be unstuffed prior to washing.

A few common styles of a pocket diaper include:
- Front pocket opening or back pocket opening or both.
- Micro-fleece liner or Microseude liner.
- Natural Fibre Inserts or Synthetics.

Example of a pocket opening with the fabric inside and PUL exterior - this is a Petite Crown diaper.

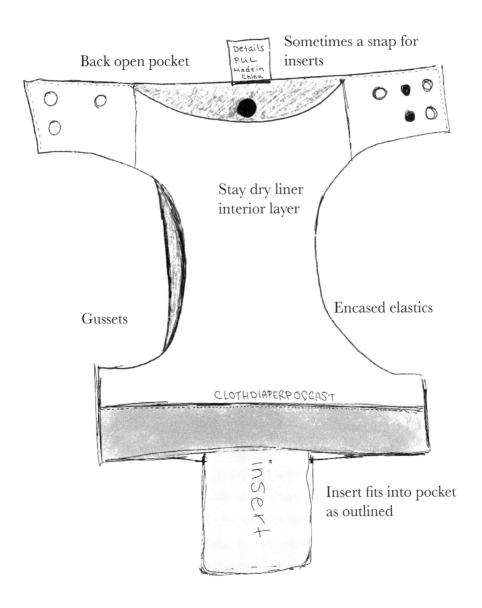

Back open pocket

Details PUL Made in China

Sometimes a snap for inserts

Stay dry liner interior layer

Gussets

Encased elastics

CLOTHDIAPERPODCAST

insert

Insert fits into pocket as outlined

Once assembled, one convenient package for all caregivers.

A pocket diaper is sold with 1-2 Microfibre inserts (sometimes bamboo or cotton, but less common). An insert is placed into the pocket opening of the diaper. Once assembled, the diaper can be put on baby. Pocket diapers are not re-used between diaper changes. Other types of absorbent material can be used instead of the provided inserts.

Microfibre inserts go inside the diaper. Microfibre cannot go against the skin because it will cause rash or irritation.

Inserts come in many shapes and sizes. Use an insert that is the right size for the size of your child. Snap them down, fold them, or use a smaller product. Longer inserts might stick out the top or back which results in leaks, bad fit, and sagging bums. A snug, trim fit close to the body is important to ensure that everything absorbs as it should.

When purchasing pocket diapers, you may get to choose the inserts, or pockets may be sold without them. Be mindful of this.

Check the description to know if you need to purchase inserts seperately. This might be to your advantage allowing you to custom choose an inser that works best for you.

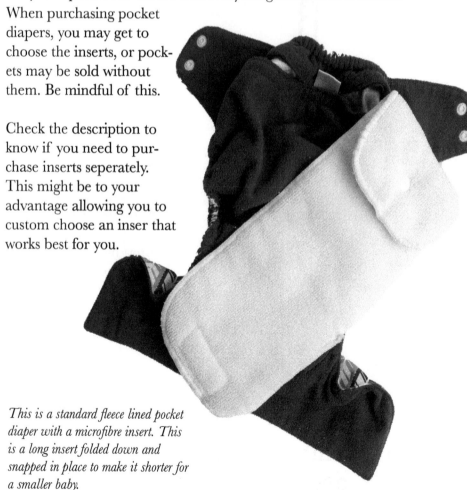

This is a standard fleece lined pocket diaper with a microfibre insert. This is a long insert folded down and snapped in place to make it shorter for a smaller baby.

A stack of pocket diapers including Bebeboo Diapers, AppleCheeks, bumGenius, les confections lili, and Nerdy Mommas. Les Confections Lili is showcased below on my daughter.

Bailey's Favourites

The pocket diaper is my least favourite cloth diaper. I find stuffing diapers to be tedious, and synthetic fibres don't work for my family.

My favourite pocket is a diaper sold with natural fibre inserts. These are often classified as an **All In Two diaper** (or snap in)**,** but the jury is out on the definition of this multi-purpose shell.

This includes: Cutie Patootie, Bebeboo, or the Lalabye Baby Diaper. These three diapers have two openings which allow inserts to agitate out in the wash with ease and no unstuffing required. I admire Thirsties and La Petite Ourse for designing functional pockets..

Please don't get caught up in the idea that pocket diapers are simple. This is a frequent conversation in the community and it's based off limited on their lifestyle and experience. All cloth diapers are simple if it works for your family - it doesn't have to be a pocket diaper to be easy.

Frequently Asked Questions about Pocket Diapers

Q: Are pocket diapers easy for people? for you?
If you pre-assemble docket diaper is given to a care provider, then it is easy to use. It's one package of everything ready for people to use, and most inserts stay place - the bonus is a pocket is cheaper than an All In One.

For you? Well, depends on how much you like stuffing inserts on laundry day. All cloth diapers require some assembly, even an All In One you need to put all the parts into the diaper.

Q: Can I use other inserts in the pocket diaper?
Yes, you can use any sort of absorbent material in the diaper. You can fold up a flat, t-shirt, receiving blanket, prefold, or anything and put it in the pocket opening. You can use inserts from other brands as well.

Q: Do I have to stuff the diaper? Can I put inserts on top?
Yes, you must stuff if you are using exposed microfibre inserts.
No, if using microfibre inserts wrapped in fleece, natural fibre inserts, or prefolds, you do not have to put the insert/absorbent material into the diaper. You can place it on the exterior of the diaper and use it like a cover.

This is your diaper. You do you.

A cotton flat on the Elemental Joy pocket diaper instead of inside, and the inserts from the Cutie Patootie diaper on top of instead of stuffed inside.

Q: My inserts are too big and/or bulky for my baby.
This happens with Microfibre inserts. You can fold the inserts down. Some inserts will have snaps for ease-of use.

If you still have difficulty with sizing, you might consider other inserts. Cheap options include re-purposing cotton towels, shirts, or receiving blankets and cutting to size (25" square, give or take) and folding them into a custom sized pad to the size of the diaper.

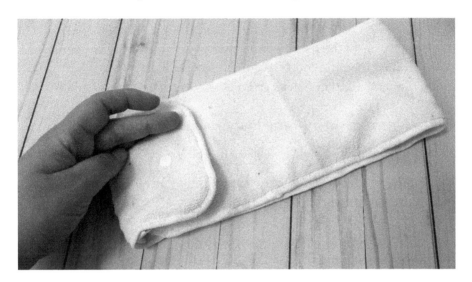

Q: Can I reuse my pocket diaper?
No, a pocket diapers is a single use cloth diaper. You put the insert into the pocket, the diaper on baby, baby soils the diaper, and the diaper is now laundry.

If you are using a prefold on top of the fleece liner, you may choose to reuse the diaper as long as the fleece does not get soiled or dirty. So maybe, but there's no hard and fast rules here people - you do what you're comfortable with.

But generally, yes, a pocket cloth diaper is used ONCE and then laundered. If you want to re-use multiple times, consider covers.

Q: Water beads up on top of the stay dry material, whats wrong?

This is normal - unless you used a petroleum based cloth diaper cream and can see visible build up. Most synthetics like fleece and micro-seude need compression to absorb the liquid from the baby side to the insert side. This compression happens with babies body, and why the diaper needs to fit close and snug to the body.

Q: My pocket diaper stinks! The interior liner, the inserts?

Synthetics like fleece and Microfibre hold smell and can be difficult to clean. If this happens try connecting with your brand or retailer. Some brands recommend occasional bleach washes for synthetic based diapers. Synthetic detergents clean synthetic fibres the best.

Q: Do I need to unstuff my diapers before putting them in the washing machine?

It depends?

Depending on the design of the diaper and your machine, you may have to remove the inserts before laundering.

Most generic pockets need to be separated.
But if your pocket has an opening at the front and the back, inserts will most likely wash out.
If the pocket opening is large and/or loose in it's structure, likely inserts will wash out.

Try it and see, or just make it habit. If you really hate touching the inners of the diapers, check and see if Diaper Dawgs has the Diaper Dawg Mitts in stock. These are handy silicone grabbers for removing soiled inserts!

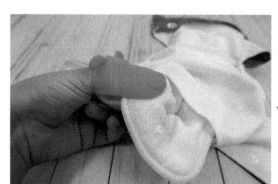

An example of the Bebeboo Diaper and Diaper Dawg mitts for removing inserts.

CLOTH DIAPER COVER

Keeps everything dry!

Abbreviation: Cover

This is a single (maybe double) layer of PUL cut into the shape of a diaper without any absorbency. You use a cloth diaper cover over a fitted, prefold or flat. Covers work with pad-folded flat/prefold and different inserts.

General Assumptions

- Newborn, Sized, One Size, Plus.
- Sold without absorbency.
- Customize your absorbency by pairing it with anything but exposed microfibre.
- Designed to be reused between changes until soiled.
- Cheaper because 1:3 ratio on absorbency to covers.
- Not stay dry.

Many different variations...
- Some have flaps.
- Some have inside snaps.
- Some don't have any.
- Some are double PUL or lined.
- Some have gussets.
- Some are low rise, or high rise.
- Some have front elastics.

Back panel for tucking inserts

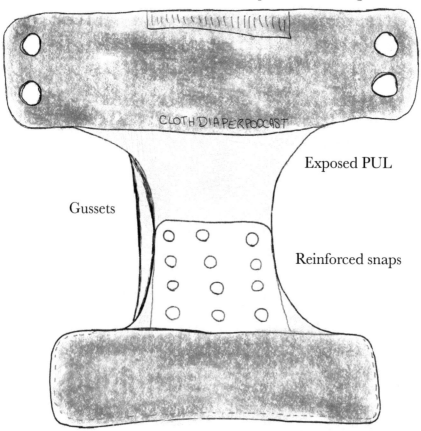

CLOTH DIAPERPODCAST

Exposed PUL

Gussets

Reinforced snaps

Front tummy
panel

Insert tucked into
the front of the
diaper

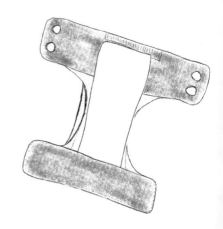

Cloth diaper covers can also be made from wool or fleece.

The cover and insert system is a low-cost cloth diaper option because a single cover can be reused multiple times per day until soiled. The cover can be wiped clean or hung to dry between changes.

To reuse: change the soiled insert for a clean/dry insert.

1 cover : 3 inserts.
Standard recommendation for the number of times a cover can be reused before washed.

Bailey's Favourites

I prefer covers with a liner or two layers of PUL because it helps reduce the impact of wash wear. I once had a machine that liked to put knicks in everything. It happens, PUL breaks down.

My favourite cover for pad-folding and inserts is something like the GroVia Hybrid cover or Flip or the Bebeboo Cover. My favourite general purpose for fitteds, flats and insert/padfolds is the Petite Crown cover or the Thirsties wraps.

Frequently Asked Questions about Covers

Q: How many inserts per cloth diaper cover?

Three inserts is the general recommendation, but reuse a cloth diaper cover as long as it's not soiled, doesn't smell, and is relatively clean. Covers with exposed PUL can be wiped clean between changes.

Q: Do my inserts have to match? Can I use a different brand? Will those inserts fit?

Most inserts will fit in other cloth diapers - unless the insert uses a patent snap, then it will not snap in. You can lay the insert in the diaper.

Inserts are interchangeable. You don't have to use Best Bottom inserts with Best Bottom shells. You can use flats, inserts, or any other product you find to absorb pee. The contour of most inserts will fit into other diapers. I have yet to find a generic insert that doesn't fit in a one size cloth diaper cover. Don't try squishing regular size inserts into newborn diapers.

Q: What's the deal with the flaps?

Depending on the diaper brand and design they are intended to hold the insert in place the same way a pocket does, without the fuss of a pocket. This is shown on the Bebeboo and Blueberry Diapers below.

You don't have to use them.

Q: How do I use a cover with a folded flat/prefold or fitted?
First, fold or fasten the absorbent material onto baby - then put the cover on baby. This is a true two step process. This will look similar to the bear below in a prefold with Boingo and Osocozy Cover.

Q: How do I keep the poop out of the elastics?
That is a hard question. There is no guarantee poop will not get onto the elastics. My suggestion: it's okay if a little ends up in the wash. If you still have poop in the elastics after wash day, try soaking the diaper.

If you use liners, allow the liner to extend out of the diaper, and then push it back into the diaper when the diaper is on baby.

Q: But I want a stay dry option without the pocket?
There's lots of options to make a cover a stay dry diaper for baby. This includes using micro-fleece, regular fleece, or athletic wicking jersey liners. These liners can be purchased from brands/retailers, or you can do-it-yourself using cheap fleece blankets, or material purchased from the store.

Q: Do all covers work for fitted diapers?
No. Some covers are designed for inserts and some are a bigger cut for fitted diapers. Some covers will be too narrow for a fitted diaper. Read reviews and recommendations before making a commitment.

WOOL COVERS
natural fibre variations

Wool is a natural fibre textile used as a cover with cloth diapering. It offers a synthetic-free variation to the cloth diaper cover. Wool is incredible because of absorbency properties, anti-bacterial properties, stay-dry properties, and lifespan. There are more amazing things to be said about wool.

Many people with reactions to elastics or PUL consider wool. Fleece covers are another alternative. They need to washed with each wear but operate in a similiar way - they don't need lano.

General Assumptions

- Knit or interlock variations.
- Typically pull on covers.
- Sized (like baby clothes).
- Use with fitted diapers or folded prefolds/flat diapers.
- More expensive.
- Handwash.
- To use as a cover, wool needs to be lanolized.

This is a pile of wool. The top two are knit wool. The light green on the bottom is an interlock wool. The bottom is a felted knit wool shortie.

Frequently Asked Questions about Wool

Q: How do I lanolize wool?
You need lanolin, soap or emulsfier, warm water, and a basin.
This is a simplified walk through of the lanolizing process.
1. Wash the wool using a gentle soap/detergent. This usually involves a short soak, followed by a rinse. Do not dry.
2. Prepare a lanolin bath by using warm water to melt a spoon of lanolin and then add an emulsifyer (or baby/wool soap). Stir this mixture until a beautiful milky colour appears.
3. Add the lanolin mixture to a basin of warm water and the clean inside-out wool. Let sit for about 20-30 minutes.
4. Squeeze out the wool, and let air dry on a flat surface.

Usually 1 tsp of lanolin per cover is the guideline for the amount you need to use. There are tutorials online to better describe this process. Some families do it in a ziploc bag. The biggest thing is to get that milky lanolin mixture and to keep the water temperature consistent.

This is an example of the milky-like colour that you want to achieve. I typically lanolize my wool in a shallow bin like this..

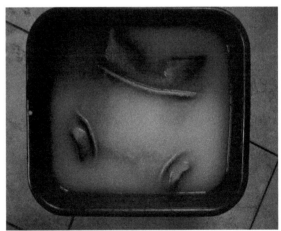

Q: Does all wool need lanolin?
No. If you're just wearing the pants as pants, then don't lano.

Q: How often do I need to lanolize wool?
When the wool cover is getting wet - then it's time to lanolize again.
Depending on your set up this might be every 3 days or once a week.

Q: Sounds like a lot of work?
Surprisingly it's not. It's pretty quick and hands-off to wash and maintain wool for diapering.

Q: What if I mess it up?

It takes a lot to ruin wool. Knit wool will begin to felt with agitation (including being worn) and with sudden changes in temperature. In my experience, this takes time and doesn't happen at once. It's harder than you think to mess wool up - mostly if someone throws knit wool in the wash, then oops. Sometimes families have success using wool conditioners to return the product to normal.

Q: Do I have to wash wool after each use?

No. Wool is magic.
Wash wool when it begins to smell.
Relanolize with each wash.

Q: Do I need special soap to was wool?

Not really. You can wash wool with gentle soaps like baby wash or a hand washing soap. Wool wash does an incredible job at washing - they tend to be gentler, conditioning, and get the grime out better.

Q: What's the best wool?

Knit wool has a beautiful stretch to it while interlock is care free. There are so many great wool makers. I recommend the affordability of Disana wool, the craftmanship of HumBird or Bumby Baby, and the custom creations you can find on Etsy.

Q: Is felted wool bad? Now what?

You can use softeners and try to relax felted wool, but it's just a smaller size. Felted wool is one of my favourite bullet-proof night time solutions. Like interlock, I feel it gives a better barrier to the wet. Felted wool is cheaper to buy second hand and a great add to my stash.

Q: Where does wool go for bedtime? What about PJs? What about clothes?

Some covers will fit under PJ's but most wont. Sloomb makes an underwoolie which is a thin wool cover that fits nicely under clothing. I usually put my kid to bed in a wool cover and long sleeve shirt and socks.

You can also buy wool pants and use them as clothes. It's just a different lifestyle for families. Join the wool groups to learn how people make it work.

SNAP IN DIAPER

That diaper no one can agree on but is also referred to as an All In Two diaper.

Abbreviation: AI2, SIO (Europe)

The definition of a Snap In Diaper depends on who you ask. I have chosen to use this term over All In Two because it tells people what they want - they want a diaper with snap in inserts. This type of diaper is one that can function in different ways (as a cover, pocket, All In One) and has internal snaps.

There are two general styles: pocket and cover.
1. Pocket versions have a pocket opening, come with natural fibre inserts, and have snaps for snapping in these inserts.

2. Cover styles are covers with snap in inserts. These are sometimes called Hybrid Diapers.

Elskbar Reusables is a popular European style Snap In Diaper that is designed to be a snap in diaper and nothing else.

General Assumptions

- Snaps inside the diaper.
- Sold with natural fibre inserts.
- Inserts feature snaps to snap into diaper cover/pocket.
- One Size, maybe newborn.
- Can be a cover, or as a pocket, or a pseudo All In One.
- Customizable because some brands carry a wide array of insert options in sizes, textiles, and absorbencies.

Frequently Asked Questions about AI2

Q: Do I have to snap in the inserts?
No, you don't have to use the snaps, or the inserts. You can mix and match as you like.

Q: Do I have to use inserts?
No, you can use prefolds, flats, anything really.

Q: Can I reuse the diaper between changes?
As long as the diaper is not soiled, dirty, or soaking wet, then reuse.

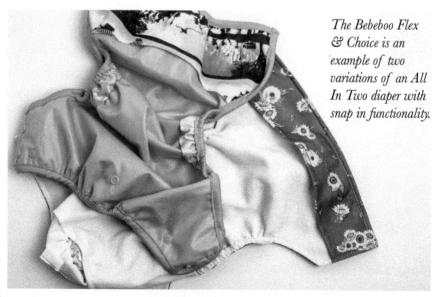

The Bebeboo Flex & Choice is an example of two variations of an All In Two diaper with snap in functionality.

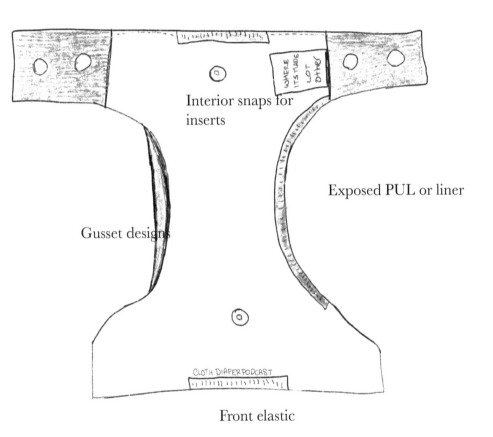

Interior snaps for inserts

Exposed PUL or liner

Gusset designs

WHERE IT'S MADE LOT OTHER

CLOTH DIAPER PODCAST

Front elastic

When assembled, one convenient package for all caregivers.

Q: Is an AI2 diaper a Hybrid?

I don't actually know. The term hybrid diaper is used differently by different brands and retailers. Some online retailers to distinguish a diaper with interchangeable inserts - this usually includes prefolds, inserts and a choice for disposable inserts. Some AI2 diapers are hybrids, but not all Hybrid diapers are AI2? Some brands call fitted diapers with built in waterproof liners hybrid diapers.

The GroVia system is typically referred to as a hybrid cloth diaper. It is sold with snap in inserts, or disposable inserts, or prefolds. It's this verstality that gives the reputation of a hybrid, but again there's really no reason why one brand chooses a term and another doesn't. Which does complicate and create confusion in the industry.

Q: Why are there different opinions on this type of diaper?

There is no governing authority on cloth diapering. Brands decide things based on knowledge and experience.

Q: What is generally preferred?

Most often people are referring to a cover with snap-in inserts when they are talking about an all in two diaper?

Cutie Patootie offers more of a pocket style system than be interchanged between functions.

Again, Elskbar, a simple cover system with snaps.

FITTED DIAPERS
A two step system

Abbreviation: Fitted Diaper

This is absorbent material sewn into the shape of a diaper with elastics and fasteners. You will need a PUL cover or a fleece/wool to keep life dry.

In some parts of the world the term Shaped or Adjusteds is used. Other terms associated: Hybrid, OBF or OBV.

General Assumptions

- Highly absorbent diapers.
- Needs a cover to be waterproof.
- Sized, OS, and Newborn.
- Natural fibres (often).
- Additional inserts/boosters available.
- Major brands and WAHM (Work At Home Mom).
- Expensive.
- Bigger, sometimes bulkier fit compared to trimmer inserts.
- Difficult to launder due to dense layers of materials.
- May shrink overtime.
- Long dry times.

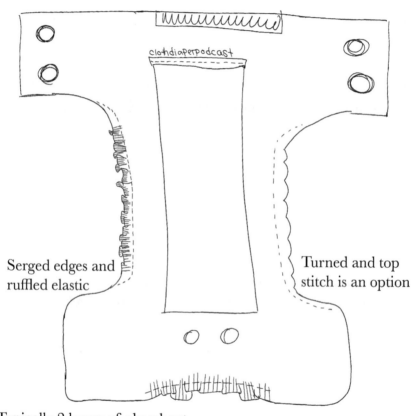

Serged edges and
ruffled elastic

Turned and top
stitch is an option

Typically 2 layers of absorbent
material in the body (inner and
outer layer)

Snaps for inserts

If you need a super duper absorbent diaper that performs well under pressure, then a fitted diaper is a good choice. A fitted diaper closely fits around the body catching pee no matter your child's body position.

To use a fitted cloth diaper, place any necessary inserts into the mid section of the diaper, then put baby onto the diaper, then fasten to baby. Once the diaper is fastened, you put on the cover. This might be pulling on a wool cover or using a cloth diaper cover. Covers can be re-used until soiled, but fitted diapers are used once and laundered.

*Fitted diapers come in two main styles of leg elastics -
either an encased elastic (turn and top stitch) as shown on the bottom
or a sewn in ruffle elastic like the top (serged elastic).*

Bailey's Favourites

My kid is a heavy wetter. Fitted diapers were my go to choice for night time diapering. Many of the brands that I used in my diapering days are no longer in business.

A few brands to check out include Lilly & Frank, Pooters Diapers, CooperRose.

If you are considering daytime fitted diapers - the Esembly Baby system is a must-have for an easy-to-use functionality.

Frequently Asked Questions about Fitted Diapers

Q: Are fitted diapers for night only?

No, many families use fitted diapers all day, and all night. The Es-embly Baby system is a great daytime system that recently came to market. Fitted diapers still need to be changed regularly throughout the day, like other diapers.

Q: What is the best fitted diaper for nights?

A fitted diaper with additional inserts or boosters and made from dense, quality textiles is your best night choice for super soakers.

Choose a product based on performance of the textile or diaper. You can learn more about the products performance by reading reviews, asking parents, and talking with the makers. Chat with fitted diaper makers to learn about their products, their reviews, and to help guide you to a product for your family. Many of these makers have years of experience tackling heavy wetter problems. They want you to succeed at cloth diapering.

Using a wool cover with a fitted diaper can give it an extra boost for a dry night. Wool holds up to30% of it's weight in moisture and when lanolized is water resistant. This is a winning combo for heavy wetters.

Q: Why are fitted diapers so expensive?

Textiles are not cheap; the labour to make a fitted cloth diaper is lengthy; and the diaper is a product of love instead of profit.

Cheap fitted diapers are available on the market, but check absorbency rankings because some might not be absorbent enough compared to highly absorbent all in one diapers, flats or prefolds. There are inserts, prefolds, or flats on the market offer better absorbency at a lower cost.

Q: My fitted diaper stinks! I can't get it clean.

Fitted diapers made with dense textiles hold on to urine. If used overnight, 8-10 hours of urine can be hard to clean. Connect with your brand for wash routine support specific to the product.

To prevent stink: rinse out fitted cloth diapers in the morning. I rinse fitted diapers by hand in the sink. Some moms toss overnight diapers in the shower and let the water run over them as they find the right shower temperature. It's multipurpose trick. Squeeze out as much water and put in wet bag. Finding a way to get the urine out quicker/ sooner can help. Allowing a diaper to dry out can reduce some of the wet-bag odor and struggles.

Q: Can I bleach wash my fitted diapers?

Check with your manufacturer for wash routine instructions. Bleach may fade colours or will leave spots if incorrectly mixed. Bleach is harsh on natural fibres and may impact the integrity of your bamboo or hemp diaper. Some communities insist no bleach use and all bleach use to be disclosed because of the impact on durability.

Some families consider sanitizing using a peroxide method. I know this isn't an answer, but it is really best to chat with the maker directly for support on what will ensure your products durability.

Q: What's with the inserts? Where do they go? Do I need them?

No. You don't need them. Some fitted diapers are sold without inserts. A fitted diaper without inserts is a great choice for daytime use.

Overnight heavy wetters may need to use inserts. This might be one booster, a specialty overnight booster, or a combo of boosters to get the right absorbency for your kid. You may find yourself mix matching between brands. That is okay.

Fitted Diapers come with many different variations of inserts. This Pooters Hemp diaper comes with one long insert and an additional booster for added absorbency. You can do whatever you want with the arrangement. Maybe you just need the booster, maybe the long, or maybe all of it and more.

NEWBORN DIAPERS
The diapers for small babies

Abbreviation: newborn

A Newborn diaper is designed for newborn babies. Newborn diapers feature a smaller cut for tiny legs and big bellies.

Preemie diapers can sometimes be found, check Etsy, and cloth diaper communities for a recommendation. This is a niche that is regularly in flux and products have come and gone over the years..

General Assumptions

- 6 - 15 lbs.
- Umbilical cord care.
- All In One, Cover, Fitted Diapers.
- Newborn sized inserts, prefolds and flats are also available.
- Absorbency on All In One is okay.
- Size 1 diapers fit newborns but don't have umbilical cut outs.
- Cost varies and depends on the value you'll get out of it. Usually around $10-15 per diaper.

This is the example of a newborn All In One diaper. Newborn fitted diapers and covers look like minis of the one size variation.

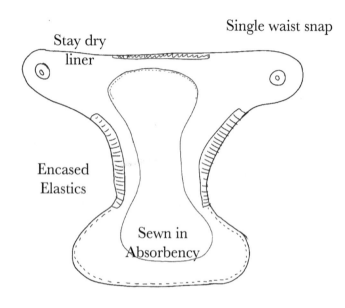

Single waist snap

Stay dry liner

Encased Elastics

Sewn in Absorbency

Middle umbilical snap. Snap one down to the other to give a divet for the umbilical stump

Pull the edges of the wing up for a tight elastic along the leg

Top for big babies

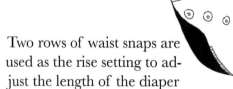

Two rows of waist snaps are used as the rise setting to adjust the length of the diaper

Bottom for Skinny legs

Bailey's Favourites

I enjoy Newborn All In One diapers. They are a trim fit for a baby and easy to use during the sleep deprived days of parenting.

I recommend checking out www.modernbottombabies.com for newborn cloth diapering advice. Her research into prefolds and covers is exceptional and would be something I would consider for another child. I highly respect Kaitlin and her approach to cloth diapering.

Do I need newborn diapers?

No. You don't have to do anything you don't want to do. I want to take a moment to remind you that you are still a cloth diapering mom if you use disposable diapers. *Cloth diapering isn't all or nothing*.

It is a hard decision to decide whether newborn diapering is the right choice for your family. I've sat in this before and been conflicted. I ended up choosing prefolds and covers for my first. This system is easier to get a custom fit on baby, but can be bulky.

Some cloth diaper rental services specialize in providing short term loans of newborn cloth diapers. This might be something to look into in your area or country.

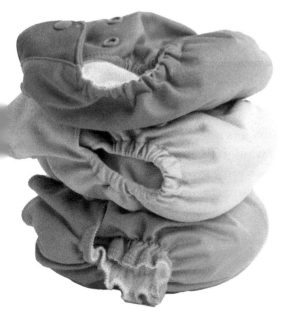

My general recommendation is... ***if you want to cloth diaper from birth,*** *consider a mixed stash of newborn diapers, size 1 covers, and smaller OS diapers.*

Smaller size diapers let you have trimmer diapers during these tiny days of diapering. Some one size diapers are massive on new babies even if the weights are right.. ***We lived in bulky diapers and unsnapped diaper shirts at home and used trimmer diapers when we left the house.***

91

5 Reasons to Not Use Newborn Cloth
1. Adjusting to motherhood is HARD.
2. Budgetary concerns.
3. Newborn baby size is unpredictable.
4. Babies can grow fast.
5. Leaky, poopy messes.

6 Reasons to Use Newborn Diapers
1. Newborn diapers give an amazing fit.
2. Second-hand diapers are cheaper.
3. It's okay to want to do this.
4. Some babies grow slow.
5. Elastics do an amazing job.
6. Newborn diapers are adorable.

Frequently Asked Questions about Newborn Diapers

Q: Will newborn diapers fit my newborn baby?

Maybe? Sorry, I can't read into the future and know your baby's size. Newborn cloth diapering gamble. This is a struggle all parents juggle.

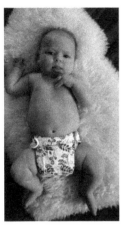

Examples of newborn cloth diapers on a 10-15lb baby. You can view more pictures at www.simplymombailey.com but this the Thirsties Newborn, Funky Fluff Newborn and KangaCare Newborn

Q: How many newborn diapers do I need?

Lots. I would recommend a starting stash of 20-25 diapers for newborn babies; whereas, with one size diapers I recommend starting with 10. Many newborn babies frequently void. A newborn can easily go through 15-20 diapers per day. Newborn babies do not like being wet.

Q: Do I need newborn fitted diapers?

Need? No.
It is nice to have as a highly absorbent diaper for naps and longer night stretches. This isn't a must-have, just a nice to have.

Q: Will baby clothes still fit?

Maybe. Cloth diapers can be bulky, especially as you learn how to use them. You might find tight fitting clothing more difficult to put on. Some families size up, some families never do. It is largely depends on the style of clothing, the style of diaper, and shape of your child. Sizing up is not a bad thing. It's just a moment in your babes life.

In my experience, I sized up for the first 6 months. Once they became a baby/toddler the diaper no longer impacted the fit of clothing. It really depends on what you put into the diaper that impacts the overall thickness - multiple microfibre inserts compared to a trim flat can be the difference in a pant size.

It's also about learning to get a good fit by placing the elastics in the crease of the leg, the snaps are folded down, and everything is as snug and secure to the body as can be. This takes practice. And girl clothing is small. My daughter never wore leggings because of that fluff bum. That's okay with me, but there are trimmer diapers that can fit under leggings including newborn all in one diapers, and super sleek one size options. Sometimes, it's about reassessing your expectations of newborn fashion goals when considering cloth diapers.

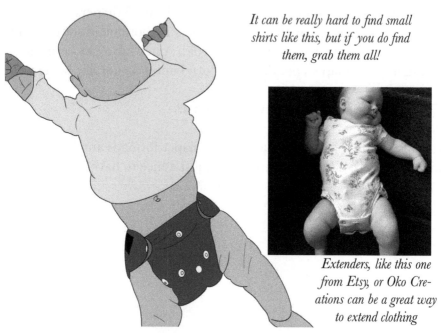

It can be really hard to find small shirts like this, but if you do find them, grab them all!

Extenders, like this one from Etsy, or Oko Creations can be a great way to extend clothing

Q: My baby hates wearing cloth diapers

Newborn babies do not like new experiences and some are fussy all the time. Make sure the diaper isn't pinching them or too tight. Then see if a stay dry diaper is a better choice, or maybe a natural fibre? Basically, try something different.

If your baby is content in disposables, but angry in cloth, I don't have suggestions. I've had this question thrown at me before. Sometimes they grow out of. It's a big adjustment post-birth. Try cloth diapering when they are happiest; don't start during witching hour.

Consider elimination communication. Be okay with regular changing.

Q: My newborn diapers are leaking!

Yes, newborns are on a liquid diet and have a lot of pee. Try changing with every pee, or more regularly, even hourly. If you still battle with leaks, newborn diapers are easily boosted using a simple cloth wipe. Newborn boosters are available, but you can also take a small cotton wipe (4-6 inches square) and fold it in half and add it to the diaper. This boost of absorbency often reduces leaks.

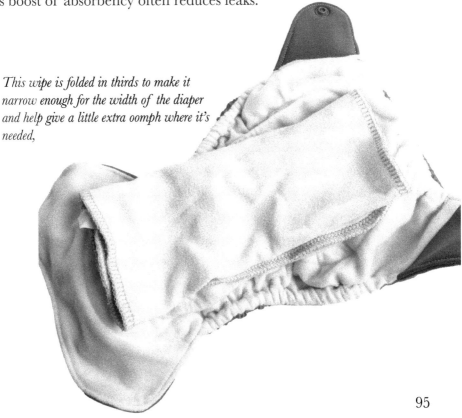

This wipe is folded in thirds to make it narrow enough for the width of the diaper and help give a little extra oomph where it's needed,

SWIM DIAPERS

The reusable diaper for everyone

A swim diapers is designed diapers for use in the pool *without any absorbency*. This is reflected in the length of the elastics, the size of the diaper, the internal mesh, the type of PUL (or lack thereof) and other quirks.

Disposable or cloth, swim diapers have one purpose and that is to keep poop out of the pool. Swim diapers do not catch pee.

General Assumptions

- Sized and one size.
- Smaller cut and tighter elastics because no absorbency is needed.
- Specifically designed for pool use.
- Wash it like a swim suit if you are not cloth diapering.

Frequently Asked Questions about Swim Diapers

Q: Can I use a delaminated diaper or other diaper?
Yes, if you can get a snug fit that keeps poop in, then you can re-purpose other diapers. *There are some worries a regular cloth diaper will fill with water and weighing down babies, but I have yet to experience that or notice it happen. Feels like a cloth diaper urban legend.*

You want the elastics to be in good working condition. You might snap the rise setting down an extra setting to fit baby.

Q: My pool requires disposable swim diapers.
Follow pool rules; however, there is ample evidence disposable swim diapers frequently fail. If you don't want to be responsible for a poop leak, feel free to double up with a cloth.

Q: How many swim diapers do I need?
Just one? This is a lifestyle question. I live in Canada and visit the pool once a month, maybe. One swim diaper works, but two might be safe because once baby poops, then you gotta leave or get a new diaper to return. Some families have multiples, and some have one.

Q: Yikes, my baby pooped in the swim diaper.
Shake it out in the toilet and launder it.
You might need to get your hands dirty and swish it all out, but wash your hands with hot water and then place the dirty diaper in a wet bag and bring it home to launder with the rest of your swim laundry.

Q: How do I wash a swim diaper?
A swim diapers is one layer of material and can be washed like a swim suit - first, remove solids. You can add it to your cloth diaper laundry, or wash it with another load of garments. You can also hand wash it and air dry in the sink if you are traveling.

Q: My baby peed all over me before we got to the pool.
Some parents will add a prefold or insert to the diaper and swap it out before they get into the pool by tucking it into a wet bag. I usually jump into the shower with baby and then dive into the pool.

TRAINING PANTS

Made with cloth, so you can wash them

Trainers, pull ups, potty pants or learners.

A training pant is a type of underwear with extra absorbency used to catch accidents during the potty learning process.

General Assumptions

- Sized, starting around 20lbs.
- PUL lined.
- Sewn in absorbency.
- Minimal absorbency (small accidents) but night options.
- Expensive product, $15-20.
- Side snaps, one size, and snap in options are available.

There are so many brands of Training pants ont the market with many different functions

Frequently Asked Questions about Trainers

Q: Will I need training pants?
Only you can answer this question. It depends on the learning process for you and your child.

Q: When did you use training pants?
I used cloth training pants when my child was confident to use the potty but would still have accidents when playing, or when we left the house. I used side snap trainers when my child still pooped in his underwear because it was easier to clean up.

Q: How much pee do training pants hold?
Cheaper training pants hold less than 5-6 ounces, just a small accident.
More expensive training pants hold 7-8 ounces, but less reliable than a diaper. Some training pants have custom inserts or work with other insert products to allow you customize the absorbency for your needs.

Q: Can I use training pants overnight?
Don't expect them to hold a nights worth of pee. Use them as a back up protection. Bed wetting sheets like the Peapod Mat or Brolly sheets are a great way to keep the bed dry and protect mattresses.

Q: How do I wash training pants?

Just like a cloth diaper.

If you have a small load, I recommend rinsing them, and washing in hot water with other small items. Many families wash training pants with other washing cloths or kitchen towels. Manufacturers will have additional wash routine support specific to their trainers.

Q: Why are they expensive?

Absorbent materials cost money. The cheaper brands on the market use less dense materializing, they aren't made in similar volumes.

Training pants vary from $10 - 25. This will depend on the quality of textiles, absorbency of the materials, and design of the product.

Bailey's Favourites

My favourite is the Sloomb trainers, followed by Thirsties & AppleCheeks.

I also liked the Omaiki side snap trainer for kids who refuse to poop on the toilet. The Mother-ease bed-wetter pant is a bulky but amazing night option that pulls on but is pricey product.

Underwear like trainers with additional absorbency and side snaps This is the Omaiki training pant.

Bebeboo also released a training pant at the end of April 2021 that features everything I love about their diapers but with stretchy side snaps and a prefold absorbency. Check out reviews and more to see if this is the next best thing in training pants.

HOW TO PUT ON A DIAPER

The same way as disposables - but not

1. Assemble the diaper. Ensure the rise snaps are in the right position, add inserts to the pocket (if you want), snap them in (if you want), fold the inserts, prefold or flat, and find any accessories like fasteners, boosters, and liners.

2. Place the widest part of the diaper under baby's bum. The back elastic is even with baby's belly button for most standard rise diapers and should cover babies bum completly. This applies to both flats, prefolds, and diapers.

3. Pass the crotch through baby's legs - while doing this the leg elastics should fall into the the crease of the leg like underwear and not sit on the thigh.

4. Pull up and hold flat against baby's belly. Depending on the rise of the diaper this might be under the belly or by the belly button.

5. Pull the back tabs around the thigh and fasten - it should not pinch or gap, and should snap smoothly in place.

6. Make any adjustments, smooth out snaps, tuck in things, and you are good.

FIT TIPS FROM A MAMA

Things to keep in mind when putting on a diaper to get a leak free experience.

The size of the insert or diaper should not overwhelm your baby. If you are on a small rise setting then use smaller inserts or fold your inserts to size. Oversized inserts lead to bulk, sag, and make it more difficult to get the leg elastics fit nicely around a baby.

Fold. Use smaller inserts. Change more often. Be creative for little babies to get that sealed fit.

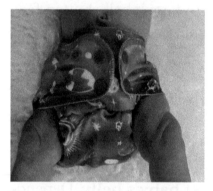

This one size diaper fits my 9 pound baby because I'm using a prefold folded at a short length to fit better and reduce bulk.

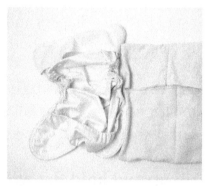

Aim to have your insert about the same length as your diaper (rise setting adjusted). You don't want it too long or too short, but to fill the shell nicely.

Uneven snaps - do it.
There's no rule that says your snaps have to be even. Wait a few weeks and baby will grow - you will not notice. Use the snap settings that work for their body shape regardless of look.

Yes, you can have a cloth diaper too tight - this will leave red marks AND lead to compression leaks. It's okay to have uneven snaps and make adjustments to give a better fit.

Rise settings and wing lifts. The rise setting makes the diaper smaller so that you can get a good fit without leaks in the legs and part of this puzzle is ensuring your insert is the right length for the size of diaper that the child needs.

If the rise setting is short enough and the inserts fit just so, try a wing lift where you pull the edge of the front panel up and over the diaper. This will create wings, or bunny ears, that stick up. Watch as you pull this front panel up and over as the leg elastics shorten and tighten into the crease of the leg. Many brands are built to do this. This is really awesome on newborn diapers.

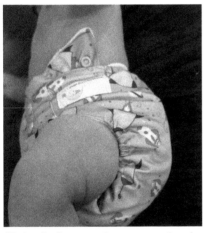

Notice the front panel corner over the edge of the diaper, that's a wing lift (using a simple tug on the front panel) to tighten around her thighs.

Play around with snaps to make a snugger fit for different shaped babies. Like snapping the hip into the wrong row.

Start higher at the belly button - In my experience this helped me avoid bum crack. I've seen other cloth diaper content creators suggest other strategies, - so, definitely play around with what works for your baby.

Start with the back elastic even with the belly button allowed the diaper to slowly move down the body as I fastened and adjusted it. It's easier to shuffle down than shuffle things back up.

Leg creases - get those elastics into the leg crease not onto the thigh and you'll have a much better fit, and mobility and function. It's hard to do with little and big babies but it really makes for a better cloth diaper experience.

If you hold the diaper in you hands like a taco or hot dog and fold the absorbency onto itself, it can be much easier to get the elastics to fall into the crease.

You want the diaper to fit like underwear.

This one size diaper fits this newborn so well because the elastics are in the leg creases. This lets her kick without leaking everywhere.

It just doesn't fit - sometimes no matter what you do the diaper will always look funny and never quite fit. If it doesn't leak, it's fine. But if it leaks then it's time to ditch and run.

It might be the diaper is poorly designed. It might be the diaper is poorly designed for their body shape. It might be the stage of life you are in. There are many different fits, styles and shapes of diapers. This is why it might be good to try a second type of diaper becuase you don't know these things until you start cloth diapering.

IT'S GOING TO BE HARD BUT NOT IMPOSSIBLE

TYPES OF ABSORBENCY

All the different things to put in a diaper

Types of Absorbency

Fitted Diapers: absorbent sewn diaper, not waterproof
Flats: single layer absorbent material
PreFlats: 2-3 layer folded flat diaper, still needs folds
Prefolds: smaller multi-layer rectangles, typically trifolded
Inserts: 2-6 layer small rectangles, usually about 2x6 inches
Boosters/Doublers: thinner, smaller inserts

FLAT DIAPERS
The original cloth diaper

A flat diaper is a single layer of absorbent textile cut into a square and then folded on a baby, or pad-folded into a diaper.

Any single layer thing is a flat - from birds-eye cotton variations, fancy stretchy flats, cut up bedsheets, and beyond. Flats are not always square.

General Assumptions

- Natural fibre - cotton or bamboo.
- Approx 27" square is regular size, smaller for newborns and larger for toddlers.
- Folded to fit baby or pad-folded in a pocket/cover.
- Cheap.

Frequently Asked Questions about Flats

Q: Can I hand wash flats?
Yes. Rinse, and wash with a small amount of detergent.

Q: Can I use flats in a pocket diaper?
Yes. Use flats with pockets, covers or to boost any other system. Fold into a pad and stuff just like an insert.

Q: Do I need stretchy flats?
If you like folding flats on, stretchy flats add that layer of luxury that gives an ease of use and glide when fastening. They tend to be a little softer because of the modal or stretchy material.

Q: Can I make my own flats?
Yes, from any sort of textile that absorbs, or can be re-purposed.

Q: What sized flats do I need?
The beauty of a flat is it can be folded to size.
Standard size is 27" square, newborn sized flats can be as small as 20"x20" and larger flats can be 30"x30" or more.

Q: How do I fold a flat cloth diaper?
Don't be scared to make your own flat folds.
Common Folds: Diaper Bag Fold, Kite Fold, Origami Fold, Pickman Fold, Twist Fold, and Padfold. To learn different types of folds, check out YouTube or Facebook for lots of great tutorials.

To padfold is to fold the material into the shape of a pad (or insert) and use like an insert.

Bailey's Favourites

I am a fan of the Osocozy cotton flats made from birds-eye material. They hand wash nicely, dry quickly, and hold up. I also loved my stash of cotton receiving blankets. I bought them used for $1/each. These absorbent blankets were custom folded into pads and used in covers for my toddler. T-shirts cut in half make a great flat.

HOW TO FOLD FLATS

A few ideas to get you started.

Flat diapers need to be folded for use. It doesn't matter how and the following pages are a few fold ideas listed for your imagination. I want you to know that you can customize any fold and make up your own. Don't worry about the perfect fold, just try.

To reduce leaks: get a nice tight line along the bum of the flat.

Loose legs lead to loose leaks. You can achieve this by pulling and moving the fabric along the body to the front wings, where it will then be fastened.

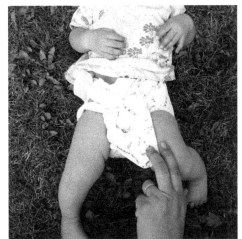

Flat folded and then a cover put over it. This fold isn't the neatest. That's okay. There's no contest.

Absorbency Location

Girls tend to wet in the mid to back of the diaper; whereas boys wet at the front. Play around with where the bulk of the absorbency is to meet the needs of your child. Not every fold will work.

You can also add boosters or inserts or double flats for increased absorbency.

The Classic Padfold

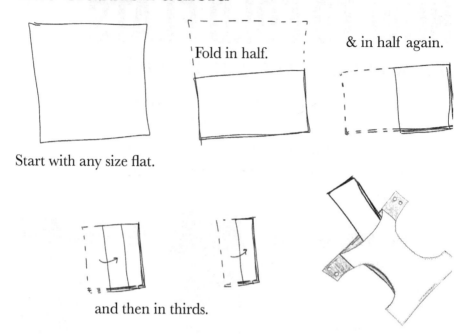

Start with any size flat.

Fold in half.

& in half again.

and then in thirds.

How to make a large flat smaller.
This is just one way to do it.

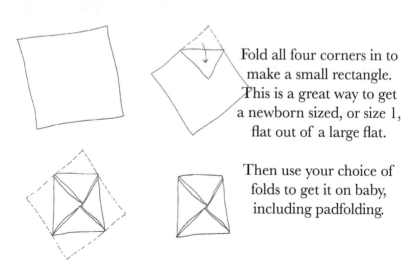

Fold all four corners in to make a small rectangle. This is a great way to get a newborn sized, or size 1, flat out of a large flat.

Then use your choice of folds to get it on baby, including padfolding.

Kite Fold

This fold gives absorbency at the front of the diaper. It is a simple and neat fold style. Adjust the length of the narrow tip depending on the size of your baby.

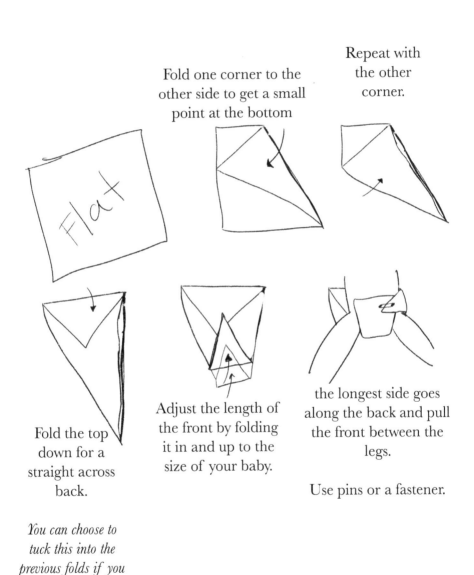

Fold one corner to the other side to get a small point at the bottom

Repeat with the other corner.

Fold the top down for a straight across back.

You can choose to tuck this into the previous folds if you want.

Adjust the length of the front by folding it in and up to the size of your baby.

the longest side goes along the back and pull the front between the legs.

Use pins or a fastener.

Pickman Fold

This fold looks intense but it gives a really trim, neat, narrow fold. You might search out some videos on it. Once you get it, you get it. Fold the corners in and then out. Then it gets folded in half, the tip is folded in, and you've got your winged flat fold.

Fold the corner in, and then fold it back onto itself out.

repeat.

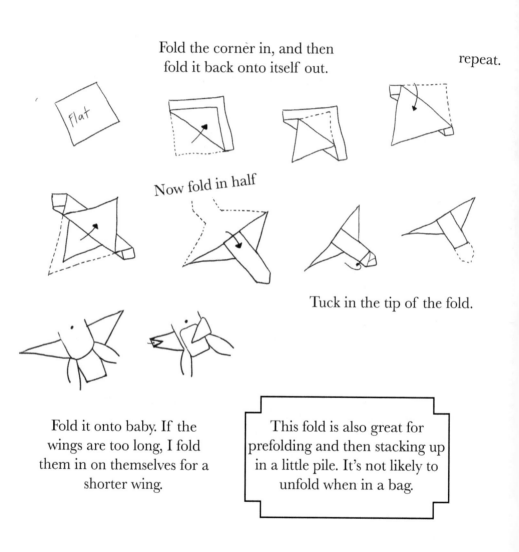

Now fold in half

Tuck in the tip of the fold.

Fold it onto baby. If the wings are too long, I fold them in on themselves for a shorter wing.

This fold is also great for prefolding and then stacking up in a little pile. It's not likely to unfold when in a bag.

Diaper Bag Fold

This fold is called the Diaper Bag Fold. A couple blogs suggest it's called this because it's easy to fold up out of the bag. The majority of the absorbency is in the front of the diaper, and the wings catch and hold poop.

Fold the sides in half to meet in the middle.

Fold the front up to the length needed.

Now fold the edges in again into the middle

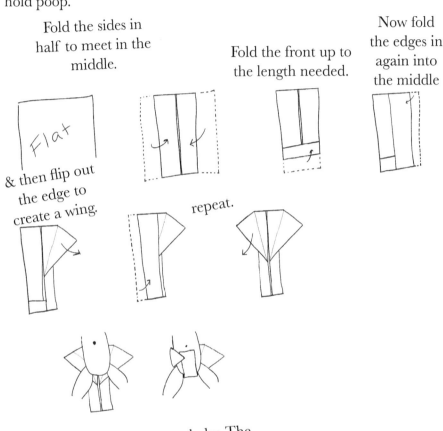

Flat

& then flip out the edge to create a wing.

repeat.

Place the diaper on baby. The opening of the wings should lay under the bottom. You may need to adjust the length as needed.

Airplane Fold

It's time to make a paper airplane out of your flat. I don't have anything else to say. I really like this fold because I'm used to making pape airplanes, so the muscle memory is there.

Fold down an inch or two (depends on how small you need the flat to be)

Now we flip it around and fold in the corners to meet in the middle.

& fold it up again into a more narrow point

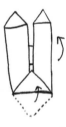

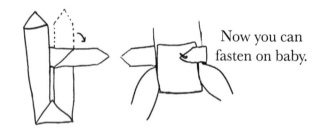

repeat, and fold in the bottom corner.

Those things poking up, you don't want that, that's the diaper wing for the waist, so fold those down to the height of the back.

Now you can fasten on baby.

Anteater Fold (Happy)

This fold has a few names. It's my favourite because I can do it on my lap. You simply fold a flat into quarters, pull out one corner, flip it over, fold up the remaining rectangle and put on baby. The "Happy variation" is when you flip the wings up for a narrower wing around bum. Feel free to jelly roll in sides or make your own variation.

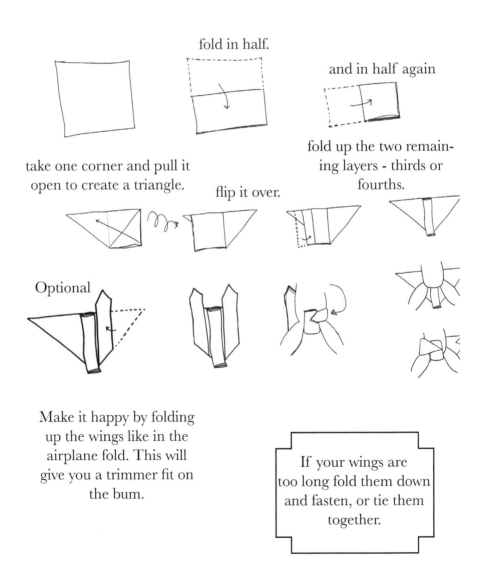

fold in half.

and in half again

take one corner and pull it open to create a triangle.

flip it over.

fold up the two remaining layers - thirds or fourths.

Optional

Make it happy by folding up the wings like in the airplane fold. This will give you a trimmer fit on the bum.

If your wings are too long fold them down and fasten, or tie them together.

PREFOLDS

Simplifying the flat diaper

Prefolds

A prefold is multiple layers of a gauze material folded into
a rectangular shape and sewn in place. A prefold diaper
is traditionally folded onto baby and fastened but can be
pad-folded and placed in a pocket, all in one, or cover.

More modern prefold styles emerged in the past decade.
These are made of only 2-3 layers of high quality fabric
sewn into a large rectangular and designed to be folded into
a pad (padfold).

General Assumptions

- Natural fibre - cotton or bamboo.
- Absorbent.
- Preemie to toddler sizes.
- Padfold and wide versions.
- Stain easily, but wash up and dry efficiently.
- Cheap.

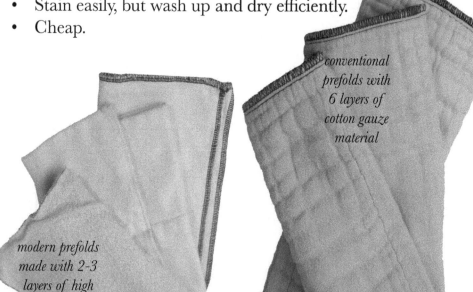

*conventional
prefolds with
6 layers of
cotton gauze
material*

*modern prefolds
made with 2-3
layers of high
quality textiles*

Frequently Asked Questions about Prefolds

Q: Can I hand wash prefolds?

Yes, but not as easily as flats. *I know it is not common, but I'm not ruling it out because natural fibres are more forgiving in washing than synthetics.*

Q: Can I use prefolds in a pocket diaper?

Yes. Use prefolds with pockets, covers or to boost any other system. Some popular all in one diapers sell prefolds as an overnight booster. You can even add it to an all in one if you please! Like I did below with the bumGenius AIO and a Hemp Babies Prefold

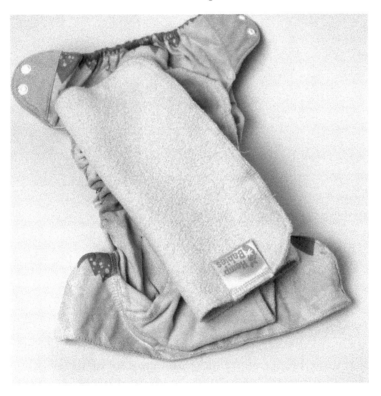

Q: What size prefold do I need?

Brands outline what size is needed to fold a diaper onto baby and these are great starting guidelines.

I prefer a size 2 prefold that measures about 8.5"x11" (give or take a few inches) for a padfold that works from kids 15-30lbs. Around 25lbs, I considered a size 3.

Q: How do I fold a prefold diaper?

There are two main options: fold it onto baby or fold into a pad. Some popular folds: Angel Fold, Bikini Fold, Jelly Roll, Newspaper or Pad-fold. These folds are diagrammed on the following pages.

  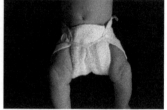

Simple padfold shown above, and to the left is a Bummis prefold done in a bikini twist with Boingo's and a simple angel fold with snappi featuring a Smart Bottoms Prefold

Q: Why are my prefolds stained?

Prefolds are made from natural fibres and stain really easily. This is easy to combat with a little sunshine. Stains are cosmetic.

Q: Do prefolds shrink? Or need to be prepped?

Yes, they do shrink when prepped and some blends will continue to shrink over time. Prepping prefolds can take a lot of work with un-bleached styles taking up to 8-10 washes to be absorbent.

Bailey's Favourites

A prefold that is 100% cotton is my favourite. I lean towards a size 2 for birth to potty training. I also like bamboo-terry prefolds. So many brands have release simple prefolds over the past few years that it's hard for me to keep up and know which is really the best. From my perspective, many are made in the same factories using the same material and just rebranded that the quest for the best is mute.

HOW TO FOLD PREFOLDS

A few ideas to get you started

Prefolds can be folded onto baby or folded into pads. More conventional prefolds or better fit styles will be more suited to padfolding. Traditional prefolds are folded onto baby and fastened using a Snappi or Boingo as shown below.

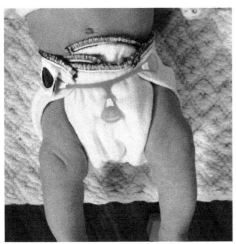

This is a simple fold with an Imagine Baby prefold and Snappi.

If you're struggling with poop leaks try folds with rolled edges. Work on a nice tight roll and then pull that roll tight across baby's bum. This can help reduce poop explosions into the cover of the diaper. A cover acts as a second line of defense to keep poop of clothing and clothes dry.

Prefolds are less likely to be prefolded and stored for use like flats. Most parents grab the prefold and roll the edges or do the folds as we are putting it on baby. There is a learning curve, but you can totally do it.

Don't forget you need a cover or waterproof exterior!

This is how the fold looks off a baby with a Boingo, GroVia Prefold and Bambino Mio Cover in a Size 2.

119

How to Padfold a Prefold

Take your prefold and fold it into thirds. Lay that prefold into a cover or put in a pocket, like shown below.

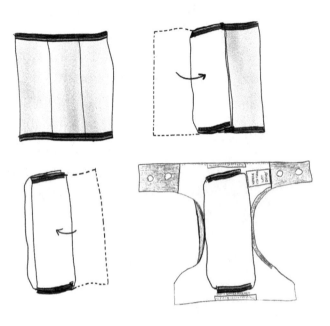

Need more absorbency?

Tuck a little something inside. Adding microfibre inserts to a prefold is a common night-strategy used by parents who love the absorbency.

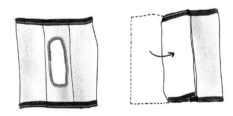

Prefold TOO Long???

You can fold a prefold to make it shorter. This is really great for front wetters (boys and tummy sleepers) because you get all the absorbency up front. Simply padfold afterwards. It can be a bulky. You can put the bulk to the back instead of the front.

OR try folding it in thirds the wrong way. This is a really good fold for girls. You get the bulk of the absorbency in the middle of the diaper. It also creates a different length that might fit bettter if your prefold is too long to be used in the conventional way.

Need something wider? Try folding your prefold in half. I want you to know you can do anything. No rules. Just catch the pee/poop.

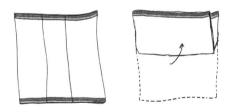

Angel Wing Fold for Prefold

Simply roll the edges to get a nicery poop barriers, but also play around with the folds, rolls, and more to get a solid fit. The prefold is simply fold it into a loose triangle so that a narrow section can pass through the legss and be fastened.

Fold in one edge.

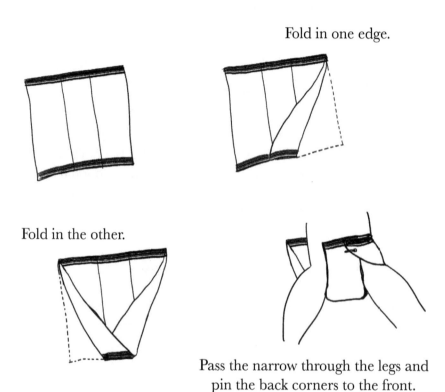

Fold in the other.

Pass the narrow through the legs and pin the back corners to the front.

Jelly Fold for a prefold

This diaper fold involves rolling the edges like a jelly roll. You'll want the back end to be wider than the front, so roll on the diagonal. You can roll with baby off the prefold or on the prefold, the rolls can come undone quickly without quick hands. The back wings are fastened to the front.

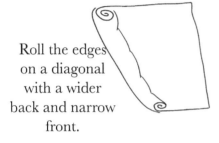

Roll the edges on a diagonal with a wider back and narrow front.

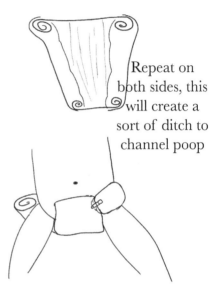

Repeat on both sides, this will create a sort of ditch to channel poop

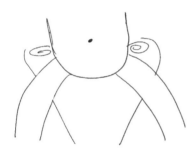

Place baby's bum on the widest section. The top of the prefold lines up with the belly button.

Pass the narrow section between the legs and hold against the belly. Fasten the back to the front.

You may find yourself needing to re-tighten the rolls along the leg.

Bikini Twist for a prefold.

This fold is twisting the prefold. This is done to create a narrow section for the crotch, and the twist creates a pocketed space for catching poop. To clean up this fold, feel free to roll or fold the edges around the bum.

Twist the diaper over on itself across the mid section.

 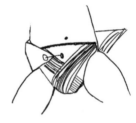

Put babies bum on the wide back end of the prefold

Pass the rest of the prefold through the legs and fasten the back wings

You may need to fold edges of the front in on itself to narrow the front panel

INSERTS

Absorbent pads for cloth diapers

An insert is a small rectangular piece of material used with a cloth diaper. An insert is 3-4" wide and 5-7."

General Assumptions

- 3-5 layers of material.
- Microfibre, cotton, bamboo or hemp blends available.
- Stay dry variations exist.
- Price depends on textile and quality.
- Absorbency depends on textile and quality.
- Some snap into diapers.
- Some have adjustable sizing using snaps to fold down.
- Some take a really long time to dry and some dry quickly.
- Can be difficult to wash.

You can mix and match brands. The exception is brands with their own patented snap size, and in that case you can't snap them in, but can still continue to use the product with the diaper system (loose, not secured).

Frequently Asked Questions about Inserts & Boosters

Q: Is more layers better? Should I get a 4 or 6 layer insert?
No, more is not always better. I don't recommend very thick inserts because they can be difficult to clean and take long to dry. Choose dense, quality textiles over multiple layers.

Q: Why are there snaps in my insert?
Some inserts have snaps to snap them down to size. If there are both male and female snaps it's to create a better shape.

Some inserts have snaps to snap them together or into a diaper. The Best Bottom Insert is being snapped into a Nerdy Mommas cover. You can find snaps at the front, back, or both on many covers, pockets, and shell style cloth diapers.

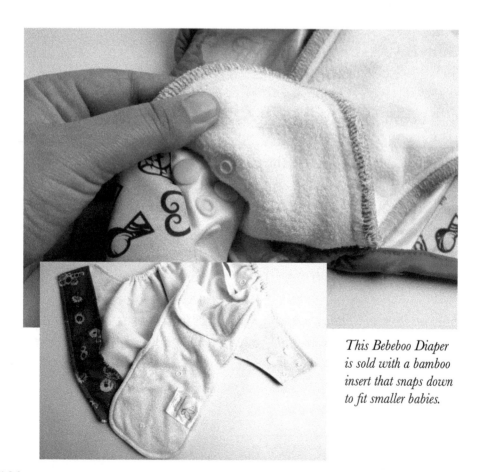

This Bebeboo Diaper is sold with a bamboo insert that snaps down to fit smaller babies.

Q: Should I layer my inserts a certain way?

Yes, and no. Hemp is often placed on the bottom because it's a slow absorber, but don't stress yourself. Microfibre is a quicker absorber but prone to compression and can't be put directly against the skin, it's usually put on the top or in the middle of inserts.

You will find a combo or layer that works best for your child. Take the picture to the left for example. Many people love the quick absorb of microfibre but struggle with compression. Pairing microfibre with a hemp booster underneath reduces leaks caused from compression and boosts performance.

Q: Can I use just one insert?

Yes. Start with one insert. If your diapers leak within 90 minutes, you probably need a second insert to last the average 2 hour span. On average, a small insert holds 4-6 ounces, and a large 6-8 ounces. This is fairly standard across most products regardless of textile.

I immediately think of the La Petite Ourse pocket diaper sold with two bamboo inserts. This is a super soaker worthy diaper - but most of us will be able to use just one insert.

Q: What about charcoal or coffee microfibre inserts?

Mostly just colouring agent, and any health claims are not verified by anyone other than the manufacturer. Many of these inserts are two layers of microfibre with two layers of coloured fleece.

This is a new trend to reduce staining and they are popular I don't have any evidence that they perform better than other synthetic products. Many times a new insert works better than an old insert.
Yes, I'm a skeptic and I'm encouraging you to do your own research to verify claims. I also believe that natural fibres work best and would encourage you to pursue those types of products.

This is a coffee fibre insert purchased off AliExpress. It advertised as a four layer insert. If you read the fine print it did say two layers of microfibre and 2 layers of microfleece. This can be deceiving if you're ordering based on headlines.

Q: What is more absorbent insert or prefolds?

Prefolds. Inserts average around 6-8 ounces at full capacity, not considering the loss in compression; whereas a prefold is 7-12 oz.

Not all prefolds are the same. If you want more information on absorbency numbers check out www.clothdiaperpodcast.com or All About Cloth Diapers. There are other lists from other creators as well. Also worthy.

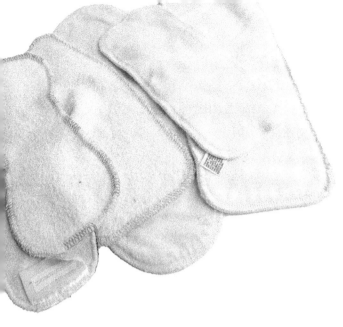

BOOSTERS/DOUBLERS

Smaller absorbent pads for cloth diapers

Thinner, smaller, pads of absorbent material intended to boost the absorbency of a cloth diaper. Add them to the top of a diaper or in a pocket, or into a prefold. Put them anywhere, with any diaper, in any combination.

General Assumptions

- 1-3 layers of material.
- Cotton or hemp (most common materials).
- Expensive cost/ounce.
- Low absorbency (less than 5 ounces).

You can be creative and use cloth wipes to boost diapers for an extra ounce or two; or cut up pieces of material like socks and more. Adding absorbency to diapers doesn't have to be fancy it can and should be simple.

Boosters can be added to a pre-existing insert. They can be added to the top, or the bottom, or sandwiched in between. Where it goes depends on the other fibres used, the set up of your diaper, and the goals you have.

A booster on top is easy to toss onto an all in one but if you have a pocket or cover system, you have the choice to optimize performance.

Many people prefer adding hemp to the bottom. Hemp is slower to absorb it does a fantastic job at capturing compression, and pulling liquid down. Cotton and bamboo boosters are verstaile and can work anywhere in the system set up.

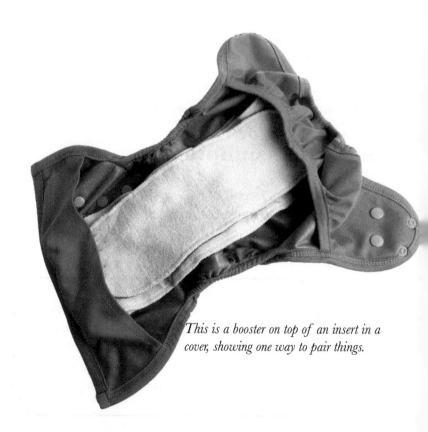

This is a booster on top of an insert in a cover, showing one way to pair things.

THE OTHER THINGS

You might find other products on the market designed to be put into a diaper or used as a diaper. This list is not exhaustive.

Just because a diaper came with an insert doesn't mean you have to use it, or that you have to snap it in, or that you have to fold it a certain way. You can replace inserts, you can create your own inserts, or you can make up your own fold styles to use them.

• Preflats - this is a contemporary prefold inspired by flats. It's often a prefold with wings in the back to allow for a easy fold onto baby. You may need a fastener.

  Preflats have really gained in popularity over the past year. They are commonly sold by work at home seamstresses (WAHM Diapers). A popular brand is Noble Bebe Diapers, and the winged preflat shown below is a hybrid flat/prefold that offers incredble absorbency and ease of use. Also check out Blythe Life Creations, she was on the podcast and shared her incredible story.

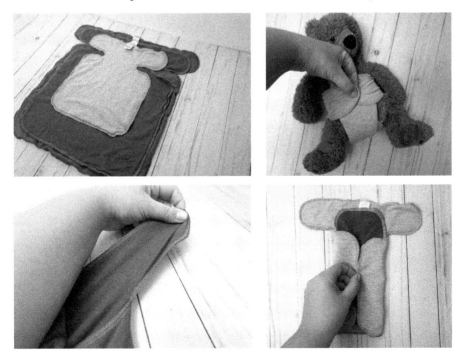

- Contours - these are typically inserts or prefolds with an hourglass shape for a different experience - very uncomon, but some hybrid versions are taking shape with the rise of the preflat.

- Flour Sack Towels (FST) - these are just kitchen towels from big box stores that are used as flats with diapers. FST is labeled "flour sack towel" in the store and usually a thinner white towel with a waffle knit or other courser feel. They are cheap and full of hype. May not be ideal for heavy wetters as they can max out around 6-9 ounces depending on the brand and weave.

- Charcoal Bamboo - this is just a synthetic textile. Read the description. Charcoal is used as a colouring agent. Many claim products like charcoal or coffee perform better or have health claims. This is not always true and often marketing hype. Be cautious with these claims and seek out 1:1 support if you need additional absorbency and feel overwhelmed.

TYPES OF CLOTH DIAPER ACCESSORIES

Just when you think you know everything, there is more. These are things you don't need but are nice to have. They are accessories. These products support families in cloth diapering.

Fasteners - Wet Bags - Liners - Cloth Wipes - Diaper Creams

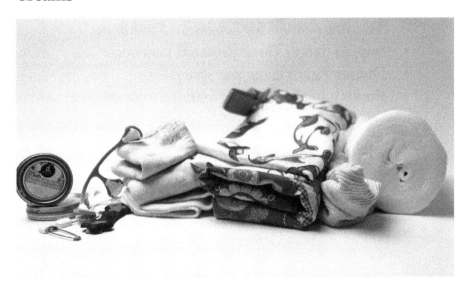

FASTENERS

Accessories for prefolds & flats

A fastener is a cloth diaper tool used to hold a prefold or flat around baby. They are sometimes used with fitted diapers (snapless variations).

You don't need to use a fastener if you quickly put on a cover. A well fitting cover will hold most diapers in place without the need for a fastener. Fasteners are helpful during the early days and for those of you not quick enough (or your baby is too quick) or if you just wanna bum around the house without a cover. You can also tie flats.

Common fasteners for flats/prefolds

- Boingo (short double prong plastic fastener). Two are needed for babies and toddlers.
- Snappi (larger three pronged fastener).
- Diaper Pins (classic pin style).
- Bands (elastic fastening bands.)

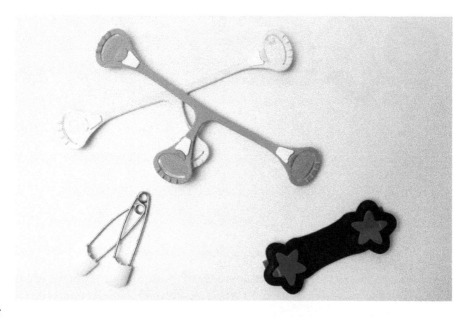

WET BAGS

Dirty diaper storage

A wet bag is a bag made out of PUL/TPU to store dirty (or clean) diapers. These bags are waterproof, but if you place soaking wet diapers in it the pressure can cause leaks.

Wet bags come in many shapes, sizes, and styles. Each brand does it a little differently to meet different needs.

Common styles
- Small with a zipper, usually holds one diaper.
- Zippered Bags - come in a variety of sizes from big to small for on-the-go.
- Diaper Pod - this is a 3 dimensional style bag that has a bottom that stands, and diapers can stand up inside. This variation holds 4-6 diapers, on average.
- Double Pocket - a secondary zippered pocket, sometimes PUL, is found on the outside. This allows you to sort clean/dirty and have two spaces for diapers in one bag.
- Hanging Wet Bag - this style is a long bag designed to hold 1-3 days worth of diapers on doorknob or hook. This diaper bag is ideal for at home.
- Diaper Pail - this bag doesn't have a zipper, usually a draw string, that can be adjusted to fit over a bucket/pail. A diaper pail is a single layer liner.

Frequently Asked Questions about Wet Bags

Q: Do I need them?
No. You can use other containers, single-use bags, and systems for storing dirty diapers at home and on the go.

Q: My wet bag stinks!
That happens. Try a few things:
1) Keep your wet bag open. Ventilation is key to breaking down the smell. So, let the diapers air out and it will make a difference
2) Don't put soaking wet diapers in the wet bag, squeeze or let them dry.
3) Don't leave the wet bag in a small confined space.
4) Rinse out heavy pee diapers.

You can also consider charcoal filters or baking soda to reduce some of the scent issues related with wet bags. Try without first.

Q: My diapers get moldy or maggots in the wet bag!
Yikes. And this is likely to happen in warm humid spaces. Try to keep your diapers dry - dry them out before piling them in the bag. Try to wash your diapers more reqularly, where possible. Connect with local parents for local-based tips for your region or weather.

I've never experienced this but I live in a cold and less humid environment.

A laundry bin or diaper pail might be a better choice? You just pile them in and it gives more space for air and breathing. Remember that not everything is going to work for every person.

Q: Why does my wet bag leak!?

PUL tries it best but if compression and too much wetness build up against it, it may begin to sweat or leak through the PUL. Avoid placing soaking wet diapers in your bag and too much compression (crammed into something or somewhere).

Q: How do I wash my wet bags?

Quick and easy! Toss them in the main wash or a cycle of towels. I don't put wet bags in the dryer. The zipper can heat up and chew up the PUL. Wet bags dry quickly.

Wet bags come in many different sizes and styles. For example the Colibri hanging wet bag and Baby Koala on-the-go style wet bag. The Colibri bag is a cotton exterior with PUL interior, the Baby Koala is double layer PUL. Different options for different budgets, styles, and needs.

Q: What about wet pails?

Wet pails, or the soaking of diapers in buckets of water (sometimes with bleach), was a common cloth diaper strategy for years. But because modern detergent and washing machines, this practice has largely been abandoned. Pre-wash cycle and a good wash routine means we don't need to soak out the pee and poop prior to laundry day.

I recommend trying dry first. If you don't have to have a bucket of water with dirty diapers soaking, that's one less thing in your house to worry about.

That said, I do meet families who insist this was a game changer. Find balance, start with the easy, and use it if you have to. But in 2020, modern washing machines with modern detergents can tackle many of the concerns related with washing. Many who handwash will consider a wet pail, but it's not my top recommendation ever because I believe there are other things we can do first to help reduce smells and get a better clean.

LINERS

for poop and wetness senstivities

A liner is a non-absorbent layer of material added to a cloth diaper for several reasons: poop removal, use of diaper creams, and/or wetness sensitivity.

Liner size will differ - typically 3-5" wide and 5-8" long and available in two sizes (small and large).

Wool liners and silk liners are used for natural healing properties. Silk is a delicate materials and is hand-wash only. Not all silk claims are verifiable, but anecdotally it is an awesome fibre. Wool liners also vary. I've never tried one but heard great things. Wool is cool like that - works as a cover and as an absorbent stay-dry liner.

Common styles
- Microfleece - stay-dry and poop removal
- Athletic Wicking Jersey - stay-dry and poop removal
- Silk - healing properties
- Wool - healing, stay-dry
- Disposable liners - poop removal

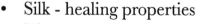

This is a silk liner on a cover and how most liners are used on a diaper.

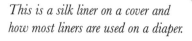

How to Use Liners

1. Lay a liner of your choice on the cloth diaper as the uppermost layer of material to go directly against baby's skin.
2. Fasten diaper onto baby.
3. Change diaper and liner. Use a new liner with each diaper change.
4. Shake poop into the toilet. If using a disposable liner, dispose in the garbage . If using a reusable liner, launder with diapers.

Lay the liner on top of the diaper

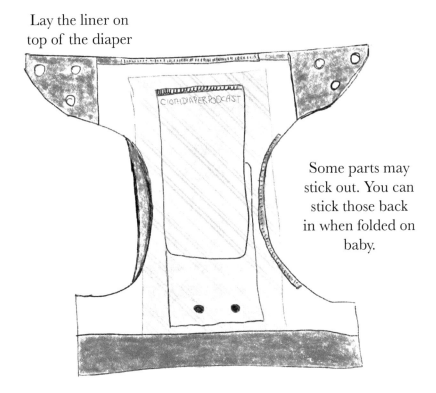

Some parts may stick out. You can stick those back in when folded on baby.

Frequently Asked Questions about Liners

Q: What is the best choice for stay-dry, or wet senstive babies?
If your child hates being wet, try a microfleece liner or AWJ (athletic wicking jersey). These materials wick moisture away from the skin and to the absorbent material under.

You can DIY (do-it-yourself) a liner by purchasing yards of material from a fabric store or repurposing materials made of microfloeece or AWJ. Many parents purchase the cheap $2-3 fleece blankets from Walmart bins to use.

Most importantly - keep your child dry! Be sure to pat dry between diaper changes. Not all screams of discomfort happen because of wetness - sometimes children don't like the feeling of peeing, sometimes children don't like the feeling of some textiles. I have met parents who went to cotton diapers and the 'wetness sensitivity' disappeared, but also met parents where fleece liners changed their life. This is about finding the answer for you and it might not be as easy as A = C.

Q: Do I need liners?
No. Liners are optional.

I like to use disposable liners when I travel for easy poop clean up. I tried microfleece liners with my son, but didn't find they made a difference in his attitutude towards being wet. In general, I have a hard time remembering to use a liner, so it's not part of my lifestyle. But many families love and embrace liners. Liners can be the difference between I can't and I can.

Q: Do I need to use a new liner every time?
Yes. It's soiled - change and dispose or launder.

Q: Can I just throw out the poopy liner?
Sure. Some families just toss the poop liners. They shake what they can into the toilet and toss. This is an added cost.

Q: What's the hardest part about liners?
Remembering to add a liner to the diaper. And it is a monthly cost.

Q: What is a silk liner used for?
Silk liners are used for their healing properties - instead of diaper cream. They are intended for short-term use to heal rashes and irritation. Silk is a natural anti-inflammatory with a stay-dry feel. Silk is handwash.

Q: What about wool liners? I thought wool prevented leaks?
Unlanolized wool is absorbent (30% of its weight), stay-dry natural fibre. They can be used in many different ways to boost performance and decrease leaks in your cloth diaper regime.

Q: Who makes the best disposable liners?
Aren't they all just the same? Yes and no.
Smart Bottoms liner is made from organic cotton and handles being washed.
GroVia is a nice wide size.

Most are made from bamboo-viscose and available in 1-2 sizes for use. Find the one that fits your budget. Start with one, and if you hate it try another.

Q: What are some liner hacks?

Some families just use Vivea brand paper towel, or paper towel, as a disposable liner.

Use liners when you anticiapte a poop if your child is on a some what regular schedule can help keep the cost down.

Q: Can I really flush disposable liners?

Eh, please don't. Many older homes and plumbers will agree that flushing other things down the toilet can cause for a plumbing head-ache. Where possible, remember to toss instead of flush. It might say flushable, but there are no guidelines around using that term.

This is an Elskbar Reusable Diaper with a disposable liner. This is how you would use the liner. It's okay if it sticks out the edges, and just tuck the liner inside the diaper after fastening to the baby.

CLOTH WIPES

for clean bums

A cloth wipe is made of an absorbent textile, like cotton or bamboo, and used to clean bums. They are used like a disposable wipe, but then washed.

They come in many shapes or sizes from about 4-6" square, and can vary in price from less than $1 per wipe to upwards of $3 per wipe depending on size, textile quality, and more.

Common styles
- Single layer or double layer
- Terry, velour, simple cotton, or flannel

I tried all the brands of cloth wipes one year and fell in love with a double thick wipe - you can find that blog post at www.simplymombailey. com.

Everyone has a different preference. Find what works for you.

How to Use Cloth Wipes

1. Wet your cloth wipes using water or a solution.
2. Clean baby's bum.
3. Shake off any poop chunks into toilet.
4. Toss into dirty diaper laundry pail.
5. Wash with diapers.

Frequently Asked Questions about Cloth Wipes

Q: Which are the best cloth wipes?

I would buy GroVia wipes (and the Thirsties) again, and again. But, they are expensive. The GroVia cloth wipe is a 2-ply terry cloth wipe does a phenomenal job cleaning up poop. Finding a wipe that works for you is navigating your budget.

- Double wipes are great if you don't like feeling the soggy-ness of mess.
- Single wipes are great if you just don't care and want the job done.
- Terry wipes are great if you like a little scrub in your wipe.
- Big wipes are great for big hands and big messes.
- Small wipes take up less space and do the job fine.

Q: How many wipes do I need?

Calculate about 1-2 wipes per change. If you like to use a lot of wipes during poopy bums, then add more. You really can't have too many wipes. They work great for noses during cold and flu season or for family cloth after all is done - that comes in handy if we ever have a toilet paper shortage again.

Start with a dozen or two.

Q: How do I store cloth wipes?
Some families store wipes in wet bags, little plastic bins like disposable wipes, or just as a pile on the counter.

Choosing to store them dry or wet is up to you. ***Wipes can be pre-moisten at the beginning of each day, but they are susceptible to going stale and sometimes moldy.*** Remember to change the water and wash out regularly.

Q: How do I use cloth wipes out of the house?
1) premoisten the wipes and put them in a small to-go container, or
2) pack them dry and moisten with a water bottle or tap in a bathroom, or
3) use a liniment or similiar booty wash product like Noleo to clean bums.

A stack of cloth wipes is a great multi-purpose item in your diaper bag. It does feel intimidating to pack them, but **you got this.** *I prefer to pack them dry and moisten with water from a bottle or bathroom sink. I'll have a mini-bottle of liniment in my bag just-in-case of sticky poops.*

Q: How do I moisten cloth wipes?
I always grabbed a handful and ran them under the bathroom tap before changing baby. This simple just-water strategy works for many parents.

If you prefer to use a cloth wipe solution, you can mix a spray bottle or perri bottle and moisten as you go by keeping it at your diaper change station. You can keep a bottle of just water at the change station. Change the water regularly to avoid mildew and stale-ness.

Or you can try a liniment, or similiar baby booty wash products.

Q: Do I need to use a cloth wipe solution?
No. Just water works for many families. A cloth wipe solution offers additional cleaning for families, as well as sooth the skin.

Q: What is a cloth wipe solution?

A cloth wipe solution is a mix of different ingredients intended to help soothe baby's bum and clean it. Cloth wipe solutions are mixed with water in some sort of bottle and the bottle is used to dampen the wipe.

Q: Can I make my own wipe solution?

Yes, using your own mix of essential oils (optional), fractioned coconut oil (or other oil), warm water, and more. You can make your own to suit you.

Q: Can I use liniment?

Yes, liniment is one of my favourite bum cleaners. Liniment is a cream used to remove stubborn things from the skin, and soothe at the same time. Limewater is a key ingredient that helps neutralize the skin from urine/poop. It also contains oils, beeswax and other simple ingredients for cleaning, soothing, and moisturizing. I used liniment with both babies when poop was stuck, or big messes needed extra clean up.

Apply directly to the wipe, and clean up baby's bum.

Canadians should check out Les Produit De Maya, and if you are American, you'll love the 3 in 1 wash product from Noleo Care. These products make cleaning the skin simple and easy to do.

Q: What is family cloth?

This is a term used when toilet paper is replaced with cloth wipes. Toilet paper and other disposable paper products create a burden on manufacturing. Many families find cloth wipes a gateway. You can wash family cloth with cloth diapers, or simply choose a hot wash cycle with detergent. This single-layer material is easy to wash and doesn't require a two-step process.

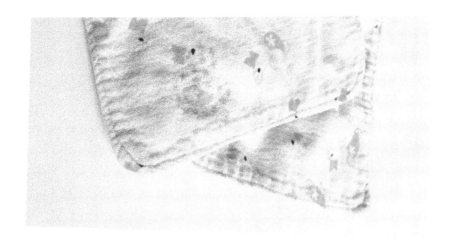

How to make your own

1. Using some sort of absorbent material like flannel sheets/ blankets, or terry-cloth material, cut into squares from 4-8" square depending on size preference. I like a bigger wipe for better coverage.

2. If the material unravels on it's own, you will need to finish the edges. You can do this by serging the edges using a serger, or tossing on a zig-zag stitch around the edges.

3. For a double layer, serge two together, or with right sides to-gether single stitch the edges leaving a one inch gap. Pull the material right-side out through this gap, and press. Add a top stitch to hold it in place.

DIAPER CREAMS
for healthy bums

Yes, you can use a diaper cream when cloth diapering. You can also use liniments or 3 in 1 products. Many parents report not needing to use creams or barriers as often when cloth diapering.

In my experience, I used rash cream with persistent bum rashes caused by teething, acidic food, or a poop that sat too long on the bum. Most other rashes clear up with regular changing and cleaning the skin.

Keeping the skin clean and dry is the best preventative measure.

Cloth diapers can be a gentle alternative to many baby skin woes related to diapering. When in doubt, check with your doctor for rash-specific advice. Some rashes can be yeast, eczema, just poop, reaction to textiles, moisture sensitivity, or a serious health issue.

The general rule for creams is: **products without petroleum - wash out of all diapers**.

Petroleum based diaper creams are less likely to wash out of synthetic diapers, but do wash out of natural-fibre diapers and eventually synthetics too.

For a while, zinc was frowned upon, but the general consensus is zinc is most likely to just stain diapers and not likely to cause clogged fibres. Zinc is a healing mineral and found in rash creams designed for the really bad bum rash. Many brands recommend using disposable liners, or even a sheet of toilet paper to reduce any potential impact to the diaper.

What do I buy or try?
Try the cloth-diaper friendly creams and ointments available at cloth diaper retailers and brands. There are many locally made products using cocoa, or mango butter, along with other oils to create soothing salves for the skin.

In a pinch, purchase what you need to and add a layer of toilet paper to your diaper to prevent it from gobbing up on the fibres and not washing out.

This is one of my favourite Canadian diaper creams from Delish Naturals. There are many fantastic small makers available at cloth diaper shops around the world.

Alternatives & FAQ

Be sure to keep baby's bum dry.
Cloth diapers are wet, the skin is moist, and the best thing I learned in my cloth diapering journey -- **take time to dry the skin between changes.**

A dry cloth to pat the skin dry helped ease a lot of irritations, and might be a trick to try yourself. This can also be achieved with Diaper Free Time.

Diaper Free Time
Diaper Free Time is term used to refer to time naked without a diaper. It is a common suggestion in the cloth community. Sometimes being in a diaper all the time is not fun for the skin. Letting the skin air dry and breathe can help heal and reduce rashes.

Diaper free time is done by removing the diaper, and letting baby hang out in the nude. You might want to do this on a waterproof mat, or pile of towels in case of accident.

Likewise, a loosely folded and pinned flat does a great job of adding air but providing some sort of protection for mobile babies. You can also take advantage to consider Elimination Communication as an addition to your diapering handbook (the practice of watching for your baby's need to eliminate and taking them to the toilet or sink).

Q: Can I use Cornstarch, Burnt Flour, or Baby Powder?
Powders can be used to help keep the skin dry. Powders are cloth safe, apply as directed. None of these products will ruin your diaper.

There is concern over talc in baby powder and respiratory health. Choose a cornstarch based powder. Please proceed with caution and under the advisment of your health officials, if this is your decision.

Burnt Flour is from an older era. It will not ruin cloth diapers.

Q: Is ABC cream cloth safe?
Maybe. There are lists on the Internet. AllAboutClothDiapers has one, and so do many others. Much too big of a topic for the extent

of this book. Most creams will wash out of most diapers, most of the time.

Q: I used ABC cream and it's stuck to my diapers!
While most things come out in the wash thanks to the power of surfactants and hot water, some things don't.

If a diaper rash caused a messy mess on the diaper, use a dish detergent, like Dawn, and spot treat the area. Scrub by hand with a brush or the textile until it lifts and removes the problem area. Rinse out under warm or hot water. Next time use a liner.

Yikes. None of that worked?
Consult with your doctor and cloth mentor for 1:1 support. Sometimes diapers do give babies a rash if they aren't properly cleaned. Sometimes babies get rashes that need medical treatment. These are big questions that are beyond my expertise.

Try to problem solve to ensure it's not your diapers wash routine. If your diapers are stink-free and smelling clean, it's unlikely to do with washing.

Try rinsing cloth diapers in a water bowl and see if the water changes colour, or becomes cloudy. Don't do this everytime, do this when you are in pickle, and some bubbles are normal - if the water turns milky then we got an issue that might be a detergent sensitivities. If this happens, it's time to troubleshoot. Troubleshooting suggestions are provided later on in this book.

Sometimes babies react to additives found in detergents. Sometimes babies react to bamboo but not cotton. There are a lot of variables that can impact babies skin and health. You'll have to be the advocate, and find the support that looks for a solution that is outside of the standard ABC formula for success.

Remember - keep the skin dry and clean. Wipe between changes, pat dry, and change frequently. Skin health can be achieved with cloth diapers.

—

you don't know till you try

—

HOW DO I CHOOSE?

It's okay to be feeling confused and over-whelmed.

Everything is going to be okay, and motherhood is full options and laying them all out like this can be a yikes moment. And we didn't even talk about the dozens of brands that create unique products for each type of diaper.

Understand why you are cloth diapering and be confident in this choice. Knowing why helps you know what you need as a consumer and parent. Because it impacts the options that I'll present to you. There are dozens of ways to cloth diaper and none of them are more right than the other.

What is the biggest priority that you can't budge on?
What needs to happen to make this work for you and what's realistic.

Write these thoughts down.
And then ask yourself, are these thoughts true?
Because girl, I know some of those thoughts are excuses and let's make sure you are being truthful to yourself about your cloth barriers.

Use these decisions and thoughts to guide you in the conversations you have and the learning you do. Be open to new ideas and be ready to bust down many myths and misconceptions because every day we learn new and different ways to cloth diaper that work for different families.

PS I have a Cloth Diaper Quiz on my Website https://www.clothdia-perpodcast.com/cloth-diaper-quiz/

First, take a moment to ask: Why are you cloth diapering?

Do you have a budget, or a lifestyle, or a consumer value that needs to be considered?

Sometimes, after all that, we think we have the perfect diaper for our why, and we mash it up to the other real-world realities and our dreams are crushed. But for every cloth diaper dream that's crushed we can find a middle ground.

If you need more help, hit me up, or chat with other cloth diaper moms. I want you to be able the ask the questions you need to get the answers to empower you to be a cloth diaper superstar.

Did you fall in love with all in one diapers only to quickly realize that's out of your $100 budget? Maybe this means you'll be scoping out the second hand market for new-to-you AIO diapers, or re-evaluating your diaper dreams.

Did you fall in love with pocket diapers, but not so sure about using synthetic inserts? There's options out there for you that use natural fibres, or maybe find pockets without inserts.

Do you need to rock that daycare life on a budget? But you also want your diapers to be made responsibly? There's brands for that.

Do you have to use laundromats? Maybe finding a simple system like covers and inserts, or flats, might be the best choice despite it not being your favourite choice.

Or maybe it's time to consider a diaper service.

Diaper services exist. This is a growing industry that offers pick up and drop off cloth diaper laundry. There might be one near you. It's an extra cost but it might be worth it if you need to cloth diaper for your child's health but you don't have the time to wash diapers.

A cloth diaper service might be the right choice for you for many other reasons, and you don't need to explain it or justify it to anyone.

There is always an answer to a problem or a need that you have.

I can't go over them all in this book, and the diversity in this is part of the reason I've held off on creating content like this. I believe that you can find the choice that works for you and your family.

Don't be scared to ask for what you want and if you need help finding a solution, reach out to someone.

I want to cloth diaper, but I have to use a laundromat...
I want to cloth diaper, but they need to be made responsibly...
I want to cloth diaper, but my child reacts to elastics...
I want to cloth diaper, but I can't afford more than $ABC..

Set the boundaries because it helps in the suggestions when you ask for help and will ensure you are set up for success. I want you to rock cloth diapering and the best way we can do that is by understanding why you are cloth diapering and what your boundaries are.

And because I don't think this gets said enough - if you really want stay on the side of crunchy, eco-friendly, environmentally savvy, consider natural fibres over synthetics. Synthetic fibres clean best with synthetic detergents. Natural fibres are a lot more forgiving when it comes to wash routines.

Buy the Pretty Cloth Diapers

If you still don't know where to start, buy the pretty diapers. That's always been my best piece of advice. If you can afford to buy them new, go into a local store and buy the pretty one's. The ones that make your heart flutter. Go online, look at the prints, and buy the one that speaks to you.

For me that's a floral, but maybe for you it's nerd-inspired prints from Nerdy Momma's.

If you can't afford to buy them new, find a second hand page and buy the pretty one's.

It's easier to cloth diaper when it brings you joy. If the sunflower diaper brings a smile to your face when you're changing your 15th diaper of the day, then buy it.

Random note about licensed prints of pop media and characters - yes, these exist but not all are legally licensed. Licensing can be expensive and that's why many big brands stick to generic or inspired prints. If you import unlicensed diapers, you could have them confiscated at the border depending on the brand and trademark policies. There are legal ramifications that some trademark owners will fight. Don't assume that all diaper prints are legally obtained. Ask questions.

HOW MANY DIAPERS?

Building your stash and buying diapers

For years, the rhetoric has been "you need 24 cloth diapers" for a complete stash. This suggestion encourages washing every third day. And it's a great suggestion if you are a stay at home mom with regular access to laundry facilities. If you're a working mom or have limited laundry facilities, then maybe it's not the best recommendation. If you're on a tight budget or a skeptic, it might not be a great recommendation. If you're having twins, or diapering a toddler, it might not be a great recommendation.

There are many exceptions to the rules, and you can make your own. Just like my recommendations listed on the following pages.

You can start with 6 diapers or 60 diapers.

How many diapers do you really need in a day??

ONE DIAPER EVERY 2HOURS FOR BABIES & TODDLERS DURING WAKING HOURS.

ONE DIAPER FOR NIGHT TIME (8-10 HOURS)

2-3 DIAPERS TO ALLOW FOR WASHING TIME

Don't forget that you will need a few diapers
while your diapers are in the wash and drying.
If you hang to dry, you might need more diapers.
Typically wash and dry can last 3-4 hours.

My Perfect Stash.

I like having a few different types of diapers in my stash because life isn't always the same and there are moments where certain diapers are just a better choice. This includes changing body shapes and absorbencies.

I washed every 2-3 days, and relied on a stash of about 24 - 30 diapers for one child. When I had two kids in diapers, my stash was about 35 diapers. I've listed below what I consider a good size stash for someone interested in washing every 3 days, and what my stash looked like.

I have had many different core stashes over the years and they have all been amazing. You can create your own style of stash. Here's some stash examples I experimented with over the years:
- 24 prefolds, 6 covers, and 3 fitted diapers
- 12 flats, 4 covers and I washed nightly (camping stash)
- 30 All In One diapers
- Newborn stash of 20 All In One, 12 fitteds, 5 covers
- Toddler nighttime stash (bed wetting days) of 6 receiving blankets and 6 big cloth diaper covers
- 2 under 2 stash of an assortment of 40 diapers.

This is a simple days worth of diapers that I used during the flats challenge and when I go camping with toddlers nine old cotton receiving blankets and 3 covers. wash and repeat.

Example of a diaper stash for 2-3 days.

3 Nighttime Diapers

This is 3 highly absorbent prefolds, or 3 fitted cloth diapers, or whatever your night strategy - it can be 3 disposables.

Pair this with 3 covers, pockets, or 1-2 pieces of wool/fleece covers.

6 All In One Diapers

I use these when I leave the house, and for other people who might be watching my kids. I just love grabbing them out of my laundry basket and tossing them in a bag to go out the door..

6 Covers & 18 Prefolds

I mostly relied on prefolds and covers for my day-to-day diapering as a stay at home mom. This was the bulk of my stash.

If you're washing every night, 7-10 diapers is a good start.
If every other night, 12-18 diapers is a good start.
If you want to wash every weekend, 32-40 day diapers, and
6-7 night diapers might be a good place to start.

You will find your flow once you get started. There is a lot of variation because every child is different. My oldest needed 10 diapers a day into toddlerhood because he would poop 3-4 times per day, and my daughter held her bladder and peed less and we used 4-6 diapers in toddlerhood. These are estimates, and just a place to start.

Newborn babies may need as many as one diaper per hour depending on frequency.

Many estimate newborns need 12-18 changes per day, including nights, as they are typically changed every time they wake up in the night. A solid newborn stash would be 20-30 diapers. You'll want 2-3 diapers per night that can hold 4-6 hours.

Build your own stash

You have different needs than me.

Think about what diapers you need to use for daycare, what diapers you need to use at home, what diapers you need to use nighttime, and then break down what you might think a good stash would be.

A good place to start is with one days worth of diapers.
You can always buy more cloth diapers. Local retailers can ship to you within a week, or you can buy them used, or you can set things away using Sezzle and lay away programs at retailers.

BUDGETING

The upfront reality check.

Different price points in cloth diapers meet different needs for different people. This means you'll find cheap diapers and expensive diapers. You can scrounge a stash for under $50 or spend over $1000 on cloth diapers.

The same is true for disposable diapering - you can spend 10 cents a disposable or 50 cents on a disposable diaper.

YOU CAN SPEND AS MUCH AS YOU WANT OR AS LITTLE AS YOU WANT ON CLOTH DIAPERS

A note on cheapies.

You may notice I haven't talked about cheap six dollar diapers from overseas and instead reiterated a conversation on cloth diaper brands and retailers. I am a strong advocate for cloth diaper retailers because they are the champions of the cloth diaper community. I'm a huge supporter of local economies and that colours the conversation in this book. I believe in people stories.

Yes, you can purchase cheapies and have a great cloth diaper experience. In my years, I have purchased them and there is a range of quality from paper thin PUL with wonky snaps, to well-built diapers. This is the gamble of ordering cloth diapers without reputations and warranty.

These experiences happen with co-op diapers, and some cloth retailers in Canada & the USA. A lot of people relabel cheap diapers - tread cautiously. Ask direct questions, rely on reviews, and think about what you are getting. We are seeing a rise of cloth diaper brands that offer products in the 10-15 USD market. This is a great ballpark for competivitley priced products that ship quickly with customer service.

 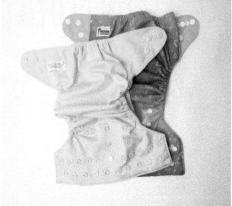

Couple Tips on Buying Direct from China

I advocate small business, but I know that many of you will make the choice for budget, values, and more to shop on AliExpress, Wish, Amazon and from co-ops to buy cheap diapers direct from wholesales overseas. Here's a few things I have learnt that I want you to know.

1. Read the descriptions carefully - cloth diaper brands will stuff the title and description with keywords. It's not uncommon to see a diaper listed as an "All In One pocket diaper cover." Look at the pictures provided and if there is a description to know what you are buying.

2. Skip the $2-3 cloth diapers - $5-7 is a sweet spot where the diaper quality begins to improve. Any diaper I've ordered for under $5 has had the thinnest PUL, the weakest snaps, insufficient stitching, and just not a diaper to set you up for success.

3. Shipping can take 6-8 weeks, and Chinese manufacturers are closed over the Chinese New Year. Not always, but it happens.

4. Consider if you need synthetic inserts - buy the cheap pockets and covers and consider matching those diapers with natural fibre flats, prefolds or upcycled products for an easier user-experience.

5. There is a difference between cheap textiles and expensive textiles when it comes to inserts and fitted diapers - the density, blend, and weave perform better and absorb better.

6. Manufacturers aren't always available to assist with cloth dipaer support and encouragement to keep you going. Many wholesales have made blantant remarks that cloth diaper support and advice is up to bloggers and other parents - not the brand. Be careful of care tags, some still promote outdated wash advise that might not work.

7. Duties & Taxes - you can expect that this might happen. It's not always, but sometimes it does. Check with your countries regulations before ordering to know what happens. For example, USA has higher import thresholds than Canadians.

How to save money

Buy diapers at new prices if you want, but if you don't, there are ways to save money. Awkward truth here, the cloth diaper mark up isn't astronomical. Cloth diaper manufacturers and retailers make very little at the end of the day after all the other responsibilities are done. Shipping is never free, it's just an added expense to someone else. Be aware of that, in your thoughts around a products value.

- **Buy second hand cloth diapers** - You can find cloth diapers posted on Facebook Marketplace, buy and sell groups specifically for baby or cloth diapers, as well as a variety of online selling platforms.

- **Re-purpose things around your home or that you can salvage.** Finding a few old t-shirts will give you more absorbency than many flats on the market and cost you even less on the dollar. If you need to do this on a budget now, re-purpose the socks, the sheets, the blankets, and anything else you can find. If it can absorb, it can be washed, dried and used as a diaper.

- **Cloth Diaper Non Profits provide diapers for low income families around the world** - this includes The Cloth Option, Jakes Diapers, Cloth for a Cause and even local-based charities across the world. They will have intake forms and support systems to get you started cloth diapering. Some brands have their own programs as well.

- **Cloth Diaper Sales** - Cloth diapers go on sale all year, but the two big sales are Black Friday & Earth Day. These sale days offer some of the biggest discounts (10-30%) and lots of other great freebies, promotions and shopping perks. Sign up for the newsletters, join the Facebook groups, and find a blogger making a list, to learn more.

- **Shop the Clearance & Seconds** - from discontinued to prints, to retailers dropping brands, clearance bins are a great way to save on diapers. Seconds are diapers that are less than perfect, but still functional.

And some words on buying second hand

Buying diapers second hand is amazing choice, but it does come with risk. Cloth diapers are not immortal and wear and tear happens: PUL breaks down, Microfibre shed, natural fibres get holes, elastics stretch out, and eventually diapers are done.

Hard Truth: Not everyone has your best interests in mind when selling diapers second hand. Many people sell stashes that have gone through many babies and don't have life left to live. Some people sell cloth diapers that have lived in smoking homes, or with the intent of spamming.

Awesome Truth: Some people try cloth diapering and they don't like that type of diaper, or it's not for them, and they sell well cared for diapers. You can find amazing deals online.

Always use PayPal for online transactions. When you purchase products with an invoice or through goods & services, you get buyer protection. It is an added cost for the seller, but it's worth it. There are scammer groups online, but there's always another scammer around the corner.

Is this a good price?

Maybe. Because cloth diapers go on sale for 20-25% a few times a years, used cloth diapers come in around 50% of retail. When they pass to a new family, they no longer have warranty and they have wear and wash history.

Each online space has their own guidelines for selling used diapers. If the diaper has been regularly used and is in good condition, then I would expect the value to be 30-50% of the original retail price, plus shipping.

In my opinion, cloth diapers that need elastics replaced, not worth anything. The work that goes into replacing elastics, plus the potential PUL breakdown is risky.

This doesn't sound optimistic, but you can find good used diapers on the second hand market. Just play smart and inquire about the potential life.

> It's just a poop catcher,
> not an investment.

Cloth diaper culture is a thing.

Many parents love the thrill of collecting all the cloth diapers. From complete rainbows to every print a brand produces, some people get a little enthusiastic about cloth diapering. *I might be one of them.*

Some brands release limited runs of products, and supply & demand does influence the market. That's why you might see some brands sold for more than retail. Drama can happen at any moment and you can loose your entire investment. Don't go into cloth diapering thinking your collecting baseball cards you can cash out in 2-3 years.

During the time it took me to write this book, I watched one brand go from above retail for used to worth nothing - it happens.

What am I looking for when buying new-to-me cloth diapers?

If I didn't scare you off, let's go shopping for used cloth diapers. There is a lot to look at. Start by checking off these boxes on the quest for second hand diapers.

1. Elastics - elastics can be replaced, sometimes. Relaxed elastics look long and loose, instead of a regular curl. Relaxing happens after a few years of heavy wear and general use. They will work for toddlers, and they will work for a period of time as they are. There is life left to be lived in relaxed elastics; just know it might not be three years of life.

2. Stains - staining is mostly cosmetic, but extensive staining may indicative of larger wash routine issues that you may or may not be ready to tackle. Proceed with caution depending on the color, fade, and type of staining on the diapers. If it looks scary, trust you gut.

3. TPU/PUL condition - You can ask for someone to take pictures of the inside PUL of the diaper so that you can see if there are noticeable defects. This is not possible with lined diapers or most AIO diapers. There is a chance you might not see knicks in a picture. Take a close look and evaluate the cost and any damage, if any.

4. Smells - cloth diapers should not smell like anything. Sometimes, you will receive diapers that are highly fragrant of detergent. My friend and I had the same wash routine and yet her diapers smelled of Tide and mine never did. It wasn't a bad thing, just a weird thing.

   Most smells will wash out in the wash. Just wash them, and if they don't begin to troubleshoot. Some smells are more challenging like smoke and pets. Tread with caution - it's okay to say no.

5. Bleach Use - I will ask about bleach because many schools of cloth diaper encourage bleach soaks and this can impact diaper health. I want to know if regular bleach washes or soaks were a thing. It's part of the wear and tear thought I'm having on the value of a used diaper.

6. Defects or Marks - ask if they haven't already been identified

7. Product Age & Use - the age of cloth diapers is a great thinking point in deciding their value and future longevity. Microfibre sheds over time, and PUL will eventually break down, and elastics will go. It's okay if that happens to you as long as you are not emotionally and financially invested in the diapers.

> Remember: when buying diapers second hand, they have lived one life already and might find their final resting place with you. Diapers don't live forever.

But you didn't ask about wash routines?
We all wash diapers differently. I don't believe the principles of a wash routines ruin diapers or make them less attractive to me as a buyer. Long soaks in bleach might ruin diapers, but everything else is just a difference of opinion. If when I receive them they are funky, then I can try to fix it, but I just incorporate them into my cloth diaper routine.

170

Estimating diaper costs

Estimating costs is hard. There are many options to diaper your child. If we look at disposable diapers, you can do it for $800 over the 2 years, or you can spend well over $2,000 in diapers buying fragrance free sustainable products. There is a range of products to meet your needs.

If you are debating between disposables or cloth for budgetary reasons, take a look at which disposable diapers you'll be buying as a family. Where will you buy them, and what is the local cost of that brand? And then compare it to a cloth diaper cost, because we all have different stories.

About my cost estimates
These numbers are based off estimated averages from cloth diaper retailers in the United States.

If you're reading this in another part of the world,
Your price structure will be different.
Canadians, expect 20-50% increase for new product,
and if a Canadians orders from a USA store,
you can be hit with duty and taxes on purchases over $50.

I'm going to break it down into cost per day. Some families need a stash of 2-3 days worth and others need a week of diapers.

Estimates are reflective of general averages amongst families. I use the average of 8-10 diapers per day to allow for a diaper change every 2 hours, plus night, plus extra because life.

171

Average Cost a day for Pocket Cloth Diapers

The average pocket cloth diaper in the United States comes in around $18 (including an insert). *Canadians expect to pay around $23 per pocket.*

Your cost is about $145-$160 per day for pocket cloth diapers with standard Microfibre inserts.

Average Cost a day for All In One Cloth Diapers

The average all in one cloth diaper is around $23 USD.
Canadians expect to pay around $30-35 per AIO cloth diaper.
This is an average microfibre inserts.

Your cost is about $180-225 per day for diapers.

Average Cost a day for Cloth Diaper Covers

The average cover is about $14 USD
Prefolds or simple flat diapers start at around $2-4 a piece.
Canadians expect to pay around $18 per cloth diaper and $3-5 for inserts.

Per day you might need 3 covers and 8-10 inserts (2-3 inserts per diaper). If you will be sending your child to daycare, expect to need a new cover/diaper for every diaper change.

Your cost is about $125-$135 per day for diapers.

This category can widely varies depending on the insert quality.
This is a great way to take advantage of higher quality inserts for heavier wetters
while paying for a cheaper diaper. Some parents buy a cover for each diaper change.

Additional Cloth Diaper Costs.

Everything is optional.

You can cloth diaper without accessories.

It just might not look as pretty or as convenient. You don't need it all, and you can pick and choose what extras work best for your life.

These prices are in American dollars for new product, other countries may be 20-30% more expensive; *looking at you Canada.*

- **Dirty diaper storage wet bag: $20-$35**
  You can use an old bucket or laundry basket to hold dirty diapers until wash day. Re-purpose an old bag.

- **Wet bag for leaving the house: $10**
  You can just toss it in a plastic grocery bag.

- **A sprayer for removing poop into the toilet: $50**
  Dunk & Swish is always free. Many families don't need a sprayer until they start solids, around 6 months.

- **Fleece liners or disposable liners: $5 per month or less.**
  An alternative to a sprayer & for sensitivities.

- **Fasteners: $12-$15**
  Looking to fold diaper onto baby whether prefolds, flats or some fitteds then you might need a fastener.

- **Nighttime diaper: $20-$50/each**
  Whether you're adding wool into the mix or investing in a high quality fitted diaper --- a night time diaper can come with a cost depending on your goals.

- **Drying rack: $20-$40**
  Drying your diapers on the line or on a rack helps extend their life. I've always put them in the dryer, but hey, many parents find this is the cats meow.

> When you bring a new baby home,
> **everything is going to increase in cost.**

Additional Household Costs.

Kids come with a lot of laundry and it doesn't really end when cloth diapering ends.

Water costs increase
Many brands suggest a 5% increase for metered water over current usage. This is less than regularly watering the lawn.

Keeping your routine simple and efficient can help keep water usage down. Don't do strips or extra rinses if you don't have to. Reach out for 1:1 support from your cloth diaper brand or retailer when you are struggling.

Electric costs increase.
Added dryer use, hot water demand, and general washing will increase electricity usage. While, washing machines are efficient at what they do, long bouts in the dryer can rack up electric bills quickly.

Again, efficient, simple routines can keep you from spending all day in the laundry room. Hanging to dry is a great cost-saving measure that also helps reduce wear and tear on cloth diapers.

Follow manufacturers wash suggestions for best practices.

I say this because it is in your best interest and because manufacturers and retailers can really help.
They know more stories, they might know your local situation better, and they are wise in experiences to share.

Extra Detergent.

You will use detergent washing cloth diapers. Using the right amount of detergent can help you save long term. Follow the manufacturers instructions for best practice on a heavily soiled load of laundry.

Detergent brands are a great resource to call/email about how to use their product most efficiently.

For reference, I use a Costco size box of powdered Tide every 3 months and I use that on everything for my family including diapers. It lasts 4-5 months now that I'm no longer cloth diapering. This box costs me $18-25 Canadian.

If you are considering eco-friendly or cloth specific detergents, you may have a different cost analysis. These products can be costly if you are not used to the cost. Remember to also consider natural fibre diapers.

Another cost consideration: sometimes diapers disappear, break, and/or fall apart.

If you buy from a brand with a warranty this might be covered, but sometimes not. These are unpredictable scenarios that have happened.

- You might need a new diaper if your dog eats it
- You might need a new diaper if your child outperforms the diapers you have or doesn't fit one size diapers in toddlerhood (otherwise known as needing more absorbency, different absorbency, or different sized cloth diapers like petite or super/plus/big).
- Daycare might throw one out.
- You might loose one.
- You might have elastics go prematurely or PUL crap out around 2 years not because you did anything but because guaranteeing something lasts forever is not practical.

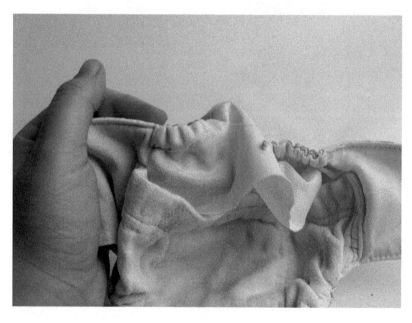

Like this time I pulled too hard trying to do up a diaper and ripped the stitching totally out of the back of this diaper. It is an easy to fix proble,, if I made the time.

IT'S JUST LAUNDRY

YOU GOT THIS.

LET'S TALK LAUNDRY

The laundry debate...

There is a lot of wash routine advice on the web, in person, and from manufacturers. There are different schools of thought on cloth diaper laundry. You will encounter a few of the big groups during your time. These conversations are oddly aggressive. They don't need to be.

I will give some basics about laundry, but this is not a recommendation, it is just information for you to consider and consult.

It's not the only way, there are other ways to wash diapers. You will find your way, but you can start here or with your manufacturer and adjust as needed. There will be different stages of diapering that change things.

I believe in simplicity and peer-supported advice. I don't subscribe to the idea of cloth diaper laundry science because what works for one family might not work for another and because there is very little publicly funded laundry science. It is very difficult to find peer-reviewed studies to back claims on the best way to tackle hard water, manage detergent levels, or tackle bleach. Many of the studies done in the field of laundry are not relevant to cloth diapering, outdated, or actually go against anecdotal suggestions about best practices. Did you know that there is research suggesting liquid is best for hard water? Yet, the common believe is powder?

We all advocate anecdotal assumptions based off our own lived experiences. But we all have a choice on whether to use this to shame and gate keep, or to empower and inform.

Sometimes things work for people, and sometimes they don't. There is not always a logical reasons why something works or doesn't work. We should fight less, and acknowledge cloth diapering looks different around the world. In an attempt to ensure everyone succeeds, I feel many groups of people leave others behind. Be open to trying new things and remember that your experiences might not work for others. Thanks for coming to my TED talk.

> **Diapers should not smell dirty when clean. We do not need to fight about the right or wrong, but instead can share our experiences gently.**
>
> **Remember kindness.**

TRUST IN YOU

You know that feeling inside of you that tells you things? Trust it.
Trust it for everything

I want you to be the master of laundry.
I want you to be able to problem solve.

You have wisdom
You can learn this and you will.

Where to get started?

Where possible follow the suggestions

of your brand or retailer, and consult for 1:1 advice.

Why? You paid for a diaper and you want your warranty. You paid for a diaper and for their customer service. These people want to help you succeed at cloth diapering, take them up for 1:1 support. This is a great way to weed out all the overwhelming information that's on the Internet and find what works for you.

Cloth diaper brands and retailers have modernized their approach and have new strategies in place to support cloth diaper parents (unlike tales of decades past. If you didn't buy your diapers from a brand or retailer directly, but used, check out their online resources, or stumble along with this book to find a basic routine that works for you.

> **Most wash routine recommendations cater to North American families with access to reliable washing facilities.**

If you need to cloth diaper differently, be cautious of helpful support from strangers on the Internet. This book mostly outlines the story of a cloth diapering family in Canada or the USA with access to a washing machine in their home. It might not be the most practical suggestion for cloth diapering in different scenarios.

If you find yourself in this scenario and find the answer to your wash routine, I would love it if you would share it with me on my Podcast or a guest blogger. Email me at bailey@clothdiaperpodcast.com.

What if I wash my cloth diapers wrong?

What if they start to smell?
We can wash them again and get rid of that stink.

What if they give my baby a rash?
We can wash them again and treat the rash.

What if they stop working?
An improper wash routine is seldom the problem for leaky diapers or poor absorption.
But, sometimes it happens and we can fix it.

What if they fall apart?
Cloth diapers shouldn't just fall apart without serious work. If you follow the wash instructions from your brand and the diaper falls apart in the first 3 months, that's not your fault. And that shouldn't happen.

What if you tried cloth diapering?
You might find joy in cloth diapering.
Your baby might never have a rash again.
You might save a lot of money not buying disposables or paying for garbage.
Maybe nothing extraordinary happens, but you did it.

USE THE DIAPERS

REMOVE THE POOP

Most formula poop, and all solid poop goes into the toilet.

REMOVE INSERTS

If they don't come out in the wash, remove them prior.

PRE WASH THE DIAPERS

Short wash to remove the bulk of the urine and remaining poop.

WASH THE DIAPERS

Long, warm or hot wash cycle with full amount of recommended detergent for load size, as per brand recommendations.

DRY THE DIAPERS

Hand diapers to dry or place in dryer on low to medium.

MAYBE FOLD THEM

& REPEAT

Poop goes in the toilet

This is the scary part. It is easy to deal with poop. Poop quickly becomes something you don't think about like you thought about it before kids. For many of us it blends into our day like our morning cup of coffee. No big.

It sounds gross.
It is gross.
Parenting is gross.
You got this.
Don't overthink.

Poop belongs in the toilet and not the landfill. It's a recommendation by most landfill authorities because septic systems are designed to effectively manage human waste byproducts.We can try to have a little less poop sitting in a landfill for the next 500 years by flushing instead of tossing when we are able.

What kind of poop goes where? And does what?

- First poops: meconimum Poop - this black tar-like substance babies poop in the first day or two. It largely just washes out in the wash. Some parents use a liner and remove the bulk of it before laundry, but most report it washing out just fine with hot water and detergent.

  You could be the exception, and I make no guarantees, I'm 2 for 2 in washing out meconium poop. When I started cloth diapering everyone said don't do it, but now people say, sure whatever.

- For cloth diapering, exclusively breastfed poop is water soluble and can be washed off in the machine. Most of us just toss these poopy diapers without doing anything to them - even if babe is on medication.

- For formula fed babies, there is grey in this conversation. For years, the general assumption is it needs to be scraped into the toilet, but some families find it is water soluble. But more and more formula families are sharing different experiences based on individual baby poop characteristics.

This varies from baby to baby, and as much as a new mom reading this will be confused, you will know when it needs to be removed and flushed.

- For babies on solids, poop goes in the toilet. All of it.

You will begin to know your kids poops very well over the coming years, and eventually they will potty train and it will be a phase of your life that is over and you might even miss it.

Don't forget:
WASH YOUR HANDS

It's all gross, but you can always wash your hands.
Warm water, soap, and some good ol' scrubbing
brings everything back to normal.

How do I remove poop?

There are many strategies for poop removal, and probably even more. Choose one that fits your budget and lifestyle.

1. **Sprayers** - or bidet wands, or shower heads, with spray nozzles that spray water with force onto the diaper pushing the poop into the toilet. Some families craft covers to keep the spray from getting everywhere, or you can check out the Diaper Dawg Cover.

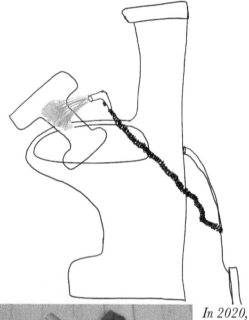

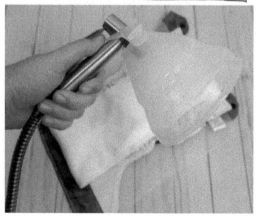

In 2020, I got to interview the creative mastermind behind the Diaper Dawg. This innovative cone covers the sprayer and reduces back spray and allows for a controlled spray as is shown on this Elskbar Reusable It is an absolutely fantastic alternative to other diaper sprayer shields and be worth considering for your family.

2. **Disposable Liners** - made of bamboo viscose, disposable liners, are thin sheets you lay on the diaper. When poop happens, the poop can be shaked into the toilet, and the liner is disposed off in the trash.

3. **Reusable Liners** - fleece liners or athletic wicking jersey are commonly used because poop slides off easily and then they can be washed. These can be purchased or made from cheap blankets in the $3 bin at Walmart or purchasing material at a fabric store.

4. **Spatulas & Spoons** - some families keep a spatula for removing off the poop into the toilet. Label it, keep it in a safe spot away from accidental playing or cooking.

5. **Dunk & Swish** - dunk the diaper into the toilet bowl and swish it around until all the poop comes off. This strategy can feel messy with your hands, but is my go-to for years. I'll let stubborn poops sit in the toilet bowl for 5 minutes and come back for a simple swish - I find the mini soak helps loosen stuck on poop that is refusing to exit. This may irritate others living in your house - so you may consider another strategy.

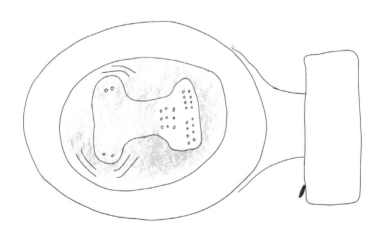

How much poop do I need to remove?
How clean does it need to be?

Try to remove as much poop as possible, but it doesn't have to be sparkling. Some detergents can handle a little poop better than others. Most wash routines can handle some residual residue.

There is a lot of trial and error in finding what works for your family. When I used a strong brand name detergent, it didn't matter how much poop came off. But when I switched to a gentle detergent I noticed I needed to get as much poop off the diaper.

In general - Don't sweat the small stuff.

WASH FAQ

Q: What kind of detergent can I use?
Start with the detergent you already use for your family.
Avoid detergents that have fabric softener added to them as fabric softeners can coat fibres and prevent absorbency in the long run.

Long lists of detergents you can and can't use can be found amongst other groups. These are made based on polls in the community, and may be reflective of a select group of people with biases and opinions. If you are concerned about your detergent, chat with your brand.

People love to hate this detergent - Rockin' Green. But why? Because someone told them it's no good and now this is one of the most hated detergents in the industry. But they've changed their formula and actively work with cloth diaper parents.

This detergent might not work for you. That's okay. It's not a reflection of the product being bad for everyone - just not a good fit for you.

Q: Can I use homemade laundry products?
Homemade detergents are frowned upon in the community and by cloth diaper brands because they are notoriously full of water softeners and lack surfactants (the thing that picks up dirt and holds it to water) to efficiently clean textiles with urine and poop with modern washing machines.

Q: What about soap nuts?
I'm not one for hard and fast rules... but this is one that I prefer to talk you out of. Soap nuts are a phenomenal idea, but when it comes to thorough washing of human feces out of diapers, it tends to fall short. They can effective for handwashing, but you really need to work at it and use hot water with agitation.

Q: My Cloth Diaper brand sells a detergent. Can I use that?
Maybe.

In 2020, I had the opportunity to chat with detergent makers and brands, and what I learnt is that cloth diaper brands and anyone who puts out a detergent, they go through a lot of work to create aformula through consults with detergent chemists and it takes years to formulate.

The product is probably a good product, and it might work for you and your diapers. Natural products are more likely to work on natural fibre diapers.

I know, from chatting with the owner, that Esembly Baby spent years to take their diaper service detergent

and create a product that can be used at home. Many cloth diaper groups argue it's just softeners - but Liz made it under consult with a detergent specialist to work and it does work for many of Esembly Baby families.

Q: Do I need to use a detergent with enzymes?
Laundry detergent doesn't NEED enzymes.

Enzymes are an additive used to help break down different fat and protein based molecules. They are really fascinating addition because they improve the cleaning efficiency and reduce staining by being a more active agent in the wash. But they are not necessary for cleaning laundry.

Most laundry detergent brands reinforce this statement - enzymes improve cleaning performance not cleaning capabilities. We have a long history of efficiently cleaning diapers with regular soap, and simple detergents. Don't get caught up in needing enzymes, but rather find a detergent that meets your needs as a consumer.

Q: Do I need to test my water?

Short answer: No.

It is nice to know your water is generally soft or generally hard. You probably know if it is hard or soft based of other soap experiences. If you spend hours in the shower rinsing your hair, you might have soft water. If this is the case, be a light handed with detergent. If your water leaves water marks and scales, then it's probably hard and you might find you need to use more detergent.

If you're struggling and nothing is going right, then ya, maybe explore it, but it's not a must-do. Don't let this keep you from starting.

Q: Do I need to use water softeners with hard water?

Short answer: No.

The best suggestion is to contact the detergent company. Over the years, I have found detergent manufacturers to be a wealth of information when it comes to using their product efficiently and effectively. Give them a call and see what they suggest for your water hardness if you're having a hard time cleaning your diapers. They do the science.

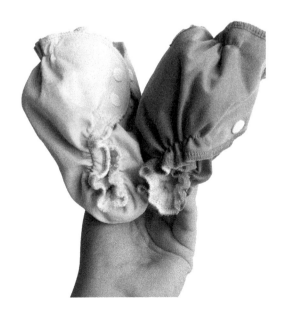

Q: Should I be concerned about mineral build up?

Maybe. In my experience working with brands, I have yet to meet a brand who has said mineral build up is a problem. You probably need rocks coming out of your taps. Don't stress about it - it's rare and usually other things are going on.

Q: I think a water softener might help things? What should I use.

I usually try adding a little more detergent first. And then would consider the other things. Borax is quite hard on your diapers. Calgon is hard to source/unavailable in Canada. Citric Acid can be expensive. Vinegar can break down washing machine seals or rubber.

If you are using a more natural detergent or things just aren't working then maybe a water softener might work. You have choices like Borax, Calgon, citric acid, vinegar, etcetera.

This is where making local friends is important. Chat with them and see what they can offer in terms of what worked for them and what didn't work for them.

PS Soft water is the hardest - finding the balance on how to use a small amount of detergent while cleaning and not getting too many suds can cause a lot of headaches.

Q: Can I use fabric softeners?

Short answer: no, many commercial products are synthetics known to coat fibres. This happens over time. You can use natural fabric softeners from brands like Mrs Meyers.

One wash with fabric softener will not ruin your diapers. Just wash again.

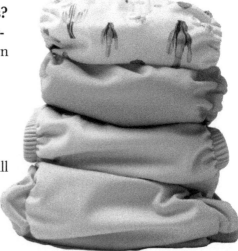

Q: Can I use vinegar in my wash?
This is a tricky question. I'm quick to say no because I don't want to be sued if you use it incorrectly. Using vinegar in a washing machine may void warranty and impact rubber seals.

Many use vinegar while hand washing cloth diapers as it softens the flats. The use of vinegar is less about the impact on diapers and more about the potential impact on machine.

Q: Can I use dryer sheets?
No. Dryer sheets coat fibres in synthetics that can cause repelling with repeated use.

One use of a dryer sheet will not ruin your diapers.
Multiple uses with time might reduce absorbency.

If a helpful partner adds a dryer sheet to a load of cloth diapers, just don't do it again. It should wash out in the next wash and not cause problems with your cloth diapers. Dryer balls are safe to use with cloth diapers.

Q: Can I use dryer balls?
Yes, dryer balls are a great way to reduce drying time and fluff up those diapers. They are totally safe to use with cloth diapers.

If you are getting a lot of static - you are likely over drying and need to shorten your dry time.

Q: What about stain sprays?
Some brands disagree with the use of optical brighteners or whiteners, so be cautious. Generally, stain sprays and like-products are safe to use with cloth diapers.

The most efficient way to treat stains is quickly removing poop, solid wash routine, and the sunshine.

Q: Can I use bleach with my diapers?
Check with the brand or retailer for instructions around bleach usage.

Long periods of soaking diapers in bleach (longer than 30 minutes, 15 minute soaks are used to sanitize) can break down fibres and textiles like PUL, cotton, and even elastics. This will shorten the lifespan.

Bleach washes are recommended for sanitizing or removing stubborn smells in synthetic diapers. Bleach is added to wash routines by some brands and can be helpful choice. Check out the recommendations by GroVia for more information on this. Washing versus soaking for long periods is the key difference in protecting your diapers.

Bleach manufacturers claim bleach works in all temperatures.

Q: Will bleach change the colour of my diapers?
PUL is colour fast, but you might get spots if splashed on. Cotton patterns and prints may fade with improper dilution.

Q: What kind of bleach can I use?
You need disinfecting or sanitizing bleach. Most laundry bleach does not meet this requirement. You are looking for the cheap simple bottle of chlorine bleach that specifies for disinfecting purposes.

Q: Do I need an agitator in my machine?
No. Washing machines without agitators are effective at cleaning clothes.

Q: My washer only has cold water...
In some parts of the world they only use cold water - washing with just cold water can be more challenging and might not get the same clean that others are experiencing.

If you choose to do this I would connect with a retailer or brand for 1:1 support. You'll likely be encouraged to find a warm water mix, but strong detergent and sun-shine dry, will be things you can do to improve your wash experience. Cold water is not ideal, but it can work for some families on a short term basis.

Q: Can I wash covers and inserts in the same machine?
Yes. Generally, wash the diaper stash with the gentlest recommenda-

tions for the gentlest diaper, or just pick one routine and go with it. If you have one product that has ABC rule and you want to abide by it, then wash all your diapers to ABC rule.

Covers and inserts can all be washed together. Many people will then hang dry covers/pockets and machine dry inserts. But for ease of life, you can wash everything together.

Q: What if all my diapers have different wash routines?
Pick the one that feels best to you and start there. Again, the gentlest wash routine might be the best place to start.

Q: Can I wash other things with my diapers?
Yes, if you're okay with them going through a hot wash, then yeah.

I have been known to fill my machine with kitchen towels, face towels, bibs, and socks. We used to say it's important to keep the items the same size as the diaper to ensure adequate agitation and laundering. However, this might be made up. Many families report washing larger items without problem. Find your common ground that works in your machine.

Q: Do I need to soak my diapers prior to washing them?
Wet pails have largely fallen out of favour. Many families successfully store dirty diapers in a wet bag or dry pail and wash on wash day. Modern washing machines, detergent, and changes in diapers has made this an unnecessary step for some families.

Q: How do I wash only a days worth of diapers?
Yes, you can wash small loads of diapers. Many families have machines that are just fine with washing 10 diapers, or they do other things if their machine really doesn't clean a small load:
1) hand wash small loads.
2) bulk up the machine with other laundry - it might be beneficial to do a handwash pre-rinse to get the majority of urine or poop out and then wash on hot with other items.
3) they have products they use to bulk - old cut up towels just for cloth diaper laundry bulking.
4) Ask around for other small load parents.

Q: Can I go a week between washing my diapers?
Yes.

Working parents around the world wash once a week. You might need to make tweaks to your routine to make it work, but you can. Some brands will disagree, and feel them out if it's important to you and read stories from other parents on how to master this wash routine.

Q: Can I wash my kids diapers in the same wash cycle?
Yes, if you are cloth diapering multiple kids you can wash them in the same washing machine. This should not be an issue for most families.

Q: What about the sanitary cycle on my machine?
Avoid using this cycle with PUL or TPU diapers. On many machines the sanitize cycle heats up the water even more and this might exceed the safe range for water temperature for your diaper PUL or TPU and cause delamination and undue wear and tear.

Q: What if I forget my diapers in the machine overnight?
Sniff test my friend. If they smell musty and bad, then a quick wash again to freshen them up. It doesn't need to be a full wash, a short cycle, maybe a tsp or tbsp of detergent and done. If they don't smell, toss them in the dryer. Musty smells tend to linger into the dryer when things have dried.

It's not unusual to do a pre-wash before bed, main wash when you wake up, and toss them in the dryer on the way to play group.

WASHING NEW CLOTH DIAPERS

The art of prepping cloth diapers

Brand new diapers need to be prepped. Prepping means to prepare them for use. Many cloth diapers use absorbent materials like organic cotton, hemp, or bamboo, they need to be washed multiple times to reach peak performance and absorbency.

Not all products need to be prepped the same. Synthetics are one wash wonder, and other products can be washed until they start to absorb. This can be a simple process. It does feel overwhelming, but when you are nesting and waiting for baby it can be oddly satisfying and enjoyable time.

Truthfully, most of us just wash a diaper once, put it on baby and hope for the best. It might not absorb, but the excitement of a new cloth diaper is something some cloth diaper parents, like myself, can't contain.

The pile of prefolds in the top corner - notice how smooth and yellow the bottom is? It hasn't been washed yet. Prefolds will fluff and soften. They might even change colour. It's harder to tell with inserts. This bamboo insert still feels tacky and if you look closely the fibres are all perfect without any shift or fluff to them. That usually changes with a wash and dry. Less sheen.

Frequently Asked Prepping Questions

Q: How do you prep cloth diapers?
Toss new cloth diapers into the machine and start washing until absorbent. If you are not currently cloth diapering, you can wash them with other loads of laundry until absorbent. It's good to toss them into the dryer every couple of washes.

Q: Do I need to wash my cloth diapers 8-10 times?
Not really. Most cloth diapers can be washed 3-4 times before use.

That said there is always an exception. For example, some products like unbleached organic cotton tend to need 8-10 washes before they begin to absorb. This is most evident with prefolds and you will be able to feel that it's still stiff and sticky.

Q: How do I know my diapers are absorbent?
Try to clean up a spilled cup of water. If it works, you're good. If it doesn't, keep washing until it does.

Q: Can I wash everything all together? Or with other clothes?
Definitely. Detergents use surfactants in which one end attaches to the oil and another to water. If your detergent is working, you shouldn't have problems with any redepositing of minerals.

Wash your new diapers with the next load of laundry, or cloth diapers. \

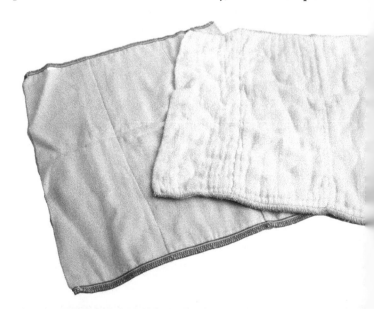

Q: Do I have to use hot water?

In my experience warm/hot water leads to better results. That said other influences impact how efficiently a product preps - like the choice of detergents, the textile, and general wash routine.

If you're washing natural fibre diapers the quickest way to prep them is hot water with a strong detergent in your washing machine.

Q: Do they need to go in the dryer?

Yes and no.

Dryers help fluff and prep the textile, but save a little work and dry every second or third wash. Some families prep their diapers by never using the dryer. Feel free to be the exception.

Many brands recommend the dryer as a step in preparing the textiles for use. The dryer helps the textiles change shape and become the magic they need to be as an absorbent material. Not all brands agree.

Q: Will my diapers shrink?

Most likely. Most cotton, bamboo, and hemp will shrink during the initial prepping process. Some products like bamboo weaves and cheaper hemp products may continue to shrink over time.

Cheaper hemp products will twist up and shrink - this is all dependent on the quality of the knit and the skills of the knitters as we learned from Geffen Baby in a recent interview. Microfibre does not shrink, but will begin to shed over time. Bamboo jersey shrinks over time.

Q: Someone suggested boiling is an efficient way to prep natural fibre cloth diapers? Like hemp and cotton?

Please don't. Boiling is really hard on the fibres and can lead to premature break down. It's also a really intensive process that requires a big pot of boiling water and prefolds - otherwise known as a mess.

In my experience boiling led to no better absorbency results. The same prefold boiled was no quicker than a few washes in the washing machine. Stick to the washing machine where possible - I don't consider boiling a viable short cut in the prepping process.

Sanitizing New-to-me Diapers

It is encouraged that new-to-you diapers be sanitized before use.
This is not a rule and not everyone does it, but a general safety pre-
caution by the community for numerous reasons.

Consider a bleach wash
A bleach wash is done by adding 1/4-1/2 cup of sanitizing bleach
during the main wash and then a rinse, and maybe another rinse, will
disinfect your diapers.

Bleach soaks over 15 minutes can be considered but any longer than
30-60 minutes can be harsh on diapers and begin to have long-term
wear issues as the material breaks down.

Most washing machines will soak clothes for 15 minutes during the
wash cycle after the bleach has been dispersed. Read your washing
machine manual to learn more and see how your machine works.

You can also soak in a bucket of diluted bleach for 15 minutes and
then wash with diapers/clothes if you'd rather not do it as a bleach
wash - reference the bottle for bleach ratios and dilution. Stir the
bleach into the water before adding the diapers.

A note about bleach
Clorox claims bleach disinfects at all water temperatures.
You will need disinfecting bleach.
Not all bleach disinfects, read the bottle.
It's typically the super cheap simple stuff.
Bleach does have a shelf life,
and can expire making it less effective as it ages.

**If used cloth diapers stink or have stains - try washing first.
If a simple wash doesn't work, then let's talk about tweaks
and stripping regimes.** Always start basic, and work your way up.

BASIC WASH ROUTINE

This is how I wash my diapers.

1. Get the diapers ready & then put them in the washing machine.

- They should be poop free (unless it's breastfed poop).
- Do not unsnap the rise settings.
- Unstuff (remove inserts) cloth diapers. *Some inserts agitate out in the wash depending on diaper design and machine.*
- Rinse heavily soiled diapers like night time or toddler pee, if stink is a lingering issue.
- You can add smaller items to your machine if you want to or need to get a full sized load. Washing one diaper at a time is not efficient or likely to clean nicely.

2. Pre-wash the diapers.

Prewashing the diapers removes the majority of the urine and poop from the material to allow clean.
The diapers come out of this cycle mostly clean.

A pre-wash cycle is typically 15-30 minutes in length on warm or cold water with a small amount of detergent (line 1, if soft water none). Choose the shortest cycle on the washing machine, it's okay if it's longer.

If you are washing with coin operated machines,
consider rinsing the diapers by hand before hand.
You can skip the pre wash at the laundromat and do it at home in the sink.

3. Wash the diapers

Now let's get them clean by using a long cycle - typically the whites cycle. The main wash does all the washing. The diapers will come out of this cycle clean.

On average, this cycle is 45 minutes long with warm or hot water and a full amount of detergent as per the detergent bottle for that load size. It's okay if its longer, it might need to be depending on how your machine works.

This is a great place to start, but there are many tweaks that can be made including water level, water temperature, detergent, and agitation to improve washing.

4. Dry the diapers

If you open the washing machine and the diapers still smell, wash them until they don't. Next time try a different routine, but smelly diapers in the dryer seem to linger.

Generally agreed upon that cloth diapers can be placed in the dryer on low until dry. Many families find medium heat is quicker, but can lead to additional wear on the textile and void warranties. Dryer balls can speed up drying.

Hanging cloth diapers is a great way to prolong their life span. Some advocate for vertical and some horizontal, and I don't have any evidence it matters. Covers and pockets typically dry in 2-3 hours, but absorbent materials can take all day or more.

And the sun! The sun is an amazing resource to help clean cloth diapers, dry them, and reduce staining. Even the winter sun in a window makes a difference.

BELIEVE YOU CAN AND YOU ARE HALF WAY THERE

Theodore Roosevelt

I DON'T THINK I CAN DO THIS...

It's normal to feel this way when you are this far into a book about cloth diapering. I bet I could write a book this long about disposables too, we are trained by three generations of disposable diaper marketing to instinctively know what we are doing when it comes to those handy little package in the grocery store.

Remember when I asked you about your why?
Why are you cloth diapering?
Remember that. Ground yourself in your values.

But what if I mess up washing the diapers?
Wash them again. Try something different.
Reach out for help. Call a friend, a retailer, or find a mama online to support you in your cloth diapering journey.

It's going to be okay, it is really hard to ruin diapers.

What if everyone around me is not into cloth diapers?
Then find people who do support you. Cloth diapering can be awesome.
It's normal for people to be scared of things they don't know about. Maybe take a moment to show them how easy it is, and point them in the direction of things you need help with - like the dishes. But it's also not your responsibility to validate their feelings or teach them to diaper.

Disposable diapers don't make motherhood easy.
There are moments of overwhelm in my life where I bought a box of disposable diapers. Life didn't get easier.
I still struggled and I still cried.
I didn't need one less load of laundry, I needed a meal or a nap, or someone else to hold the screaming children.

It's also okay to stop cloth diapering and start disposable diapering. You don't have to cloth diaper full time to be a cloth diaper parent. You are allowed to take breaks. Return when you are ready.

MY DIAPERS SMELL!

They shouldn't smell.

If cloth diapers smell after wash day or while on the bum (in like a bad way, not a fresh pee or poop way) --- then something is up. This is the moment of panic for every cloth diapering parent.

You might want to give up.
I have been there my friend. I have wanted to give up because of a persistent smell issue and the frustration of figuring it out.
But we can do this. You can do this.
It's just a hiccup.

The common cloth diaper rhetoric is that you should NEVER have to strip your diapers with a good wash routine. I call baloney on this idea that if you need to strip or reset your diapers that your wash routine is BAD. Normalize that human error happens. Needing to strip or reset your diapers isn't an immediate failure, but rather an acceptance that something isn't working. We're only human. It happens to the best of us.

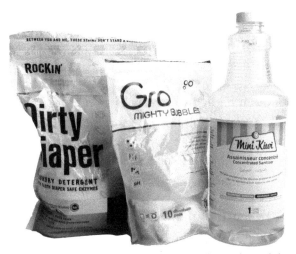

Some product examples that can be used to strip or reset diapers beyond detergent include Dirty Diaper by Rockin' Green, GroVia Mighty Bubbles, Mini Kiwi Sanitizer. These materials are designed to help fight stink and smells built up in diapers.

Need some real life stories of parents defeating stinks and smells? Check out the parent guests on the Cloth Diaper Podcast. They share stories of struggle and triumph in finding a wash routine solution that worked for them. You got this.

If you get a smell: Start small. Ask Questions. Consider small tweaks. We don't need to immediately jump to a new plan from scratch.

I don't want to say it's normal to have smells, but it's not uncommon. Sometimes it's a change in diet, sometimes it was a mistake with the detergent or the wash temperature, sometimes the routine really doesn't work for the type of diapers, type of water, type of machine, and more.

There are two main cloth diaper smells: barnyard and ammonia.

If you are struggling please reach out to a cloth diaper brand or retailer for 1:1 support to help understand your specific situation and experience. These are suggestions based off my limited experience as a cloth diaper consultant and advisor for the past five years. There are always new situations that need different answers. I find the more I know, the less I know and the more I want to connect parents with others with lived experiences.

That Barnyard Smell
Think of a smelly barn and that's your smell.

Barnyard smell often happens when poop is not adequately cleaned from the textiles. You might not see it, and it might just sneak up with time. Sometimes a round in the dryer and you smell it, sometimes when baby pees. It might come after a week of diarrhea or heavy pooping.

A simple fix for barnyard is to try one of these adjustments: remove poop more thoroughly from the diaper before wash day, more agitation (longer wash cycles to remove the poop), more detergent (maybe your ratio to load size and dirtiness was off), or different water temperature (better open fibres to clean out the dirt).

Those Ammonia Smells

This smell is potent pee, it might even make your eyes water.

Ammonia smells sometimes come with angry red rashes across the entire diaper section (anywhere the skin is wet). Ammonia is often associated with using too much detergent or not getting all the pee out of the textiles (especially in dense diapers used at night or/and for toddlers).

To check for excess detergent, taken an insert and place it in a bowl of water. If the water becomes obviously cloudy, or very sudsy, then it is time to kick out the detergent. Keep rinsing with hot or warm water till it is gone. The next stage is change your routine - use less detergent, or maybe an extra rinse cycle Don't be swishing inserts all the time, just when life gets bad. K?

- Ammonia can also happen with changes in baby's age and diet.
- Ammonia can also happen when you're not washing the pee out because of agitation or water temperature.
- Ammonia can happen for many reasons.

For example, I got ammonia, and
the solution was an extra rinse every 2-3 washes.
I tried using less, but then I got barnyard.
Sometimes the answer isn't neat and tidy.
Sometimes the answer is little changes here and there.

You will need to experiment. You can chat 1:1 with a brand, or a local parent and see if there are other ideas for kicking the smell.

Other Smells?

Smells can be hard to tackle. They come and they go. You might not understand why or what, but you can try to fix them.

You will be able to fix the problems.
You are strong, capable, and wise.

These are other problem-solving strategies that work for parents when battling stink in cloth diapers.

- Wash your diapers with 1.5-2x the detergent you normally use. Extra kick of detergent, with a thorough rinse can sometimes work like a simple easy-to use strip.

- Clean your washing machine! It should be cleaned monthly using bleach or washing machine products. Check your manual for additional support and how-to.

- Sun your diapers regularly. The sun is amazing at cleaning. In some parts of the world they only wash with cold but rely on the sun to keep their diapers stink free.

- Add 1/8 cup or 1/4 cup of bleach to your wash cycle semi-regularly to combat smells. This is particularly handy with synthetic diapers. Not all brands agree, but some do recommend this strategy.

- Try GroVia Mighty Bubbles - This simple cleaning agent does a great job of resetting diapers. Follow the package instructions and only use as needed.

Try making changes to your routine before stripping. Often washing your diapers better the next time can kick it out.

STRIPPING DIAPERS

Not the club, the laundry room

Cloth Diaper Strip

To strip cloth diapers means to use a chemical solution to remove minerals and deposits from the diaper.

There are different ways to do this from DIY solutions to products you might purchase like GroVia Mighty Bubbles or RLR.

Stripping is considered a last resort because simple tweaks in your routine should be your first line of defense to tackling stink.

My favourite way to reset diapers is to use double the detergent, specifically using Tide; it is a strong detergent that does an amazing job of cleaning diapers. Tide is not the most environmentally friendly of products but it works, and it's a choice that you can make for your family. GroVia Mighty Bubbles is a great product when you follow the package directions. It is incredible simple and straight forward.

Q: When do I need to strip?

When simple changes to your routine don't make things better. When you feel overwhelmed and don't know what else to do to kick a smell or tackle an issue.

I have needed to tweak and strip diapers because I'm an imperfect human. Sometimes I got sloppy with my detergent, and sometimes my kids became toddlers with strong pee or lots of poop. These moments - I tried to do tweaks, wash in double detergent, but maybe it didn't work so I busted out a bag of GroVia Mighty Bubbles. In these life moments, I relied on a strip to reset my cloth diapers. I usually went back to the same routine because it works 90% of the time.

STAINS HAPPEN

It's a poop catcher after all

A stained cloth diaper is a normal unsightly problem. If there is no poop in the fibres of the diaper, then it's just a stain and not a cleaning problem. Stains happen, they happen to all textiles when something with pigment sits a little longer than it should have.

Some scenarios are more likely to cause staining than others.

- Natural fibre diapers like cotton, bamboo and hemp are more likely to stain.
- Tight weave textiles over terry fibres seem to hold stains.
- Breastfed poop stains natural fibres with a bright yellow mustard.
- If poop sits on a diaper for a long time, it can leave a stain.
- Some foods influence stains more than others: spaghetti, blueberry, dyed medication, or beets, to think of a few.
- Detergents free of enzymes, optical brighteners, whiteners, or other stain fighting additives can leave diapers more prone to staining.

Stains are harmless. They will not hurt your baby. They can be time consuming and expensive to treat. It is okay to ignore them.

Q; How do I get rid of stains?
Here's a few strategies for tackling stains. Some stains may never disappear.

- Sunshine is amazing and you can use it all year round. Place wet or damp diapers outside or in a window and watch stains fade away. This works for a lot of simple stains that have been washed once but may not work for deeper set in stains.

  Yes, you can do this with winter sun or summer sun.

- Commercial stain removal products from the store can be used to pre-treat diapers or treat set in stains. Most products are cloth safe, this can be an expensive strategy for stain treatment.

- Try using a detergent with enzymes, and/or additives like optical brighteners and whiteners can fade stains and reduce overall staining if it is a recurrent issue. Some people have luck with products like GroVia Mighty Bubbles for stains.

- Time fades many stains. My newborn diapers were stained early on but in a few months the stains had faded.

Q; What about stained PUL?
Many people find PUL or TPU is fairly stain resistant to most things. It's rare to get a persistent stain, especially on higher quality PULs (but not always - they can stain too). Sometimes PUL will begin to yellow with age, again not much can be done with that.

Spaghetti and other tomato products are known to stain PUL and it can be a bugger to get off. The sun usually fades it but not always.

I also know that if your husband leaves a pen in the dryer, it will explode and you'll almost never get that out of the PUL. I think it's a nice look with a story now. Ink is a hard stain to remove.

HAND WASHING CLOTH
Keep it simple

I learnt to hand wash cloth diapers because of the Flats & Handwashing challenge - an annual event put on to spread awareness about the possibilty of cloth diapers in all situations that still goes on and is hosted by the Cloth Diaper Podcast. Find the group on Facebook.

Learning to hand wash cloth diapers is an experience. It taught me the basics of laundry and the simplicity of cloth diapering. Knowing how to hand wash cloth diapers is a survival task. If you are ever in a crisis situation this can be handy - it can be hard to source disposable diapers and so washing with what you have can keep baby's bum healthy.

What do you need? You really don't need anything but soap or detergent and your hands - and water. Yes, you can get buckets, gizmos, plungers and more. These are tools to help you and make it easier.

How do I do it? Using water and very little soap/detergent you're going to scrub your diapers till they are clean.

Okay, there is a little more to that. It's the same process as machine washing your diapers. Soak your diapers - scrub, rinse & repeat.

- Soaking helps the yuck leave.
- Scrubbing gets the yuck to leave.
- Rinsing removes the soap.

Repeat because the first time is usually not clean enough.

Then hang to dry.

This plunger and bucket method is a classic strategy for washing diapers.

Frequently Asked Questions About Handwashing

Q: Why can I use soap?
Handwashing lends itself to soap nicely - it's the original laundry cleaner. Detergent was invented for washing machines and synthetic textiles. Prior, we used soap. Soap is grated or rubbed into clothing and removes dirt particles from the textile.

Issues like soap scum are less prevelant with handwashing because of the entire process. If it becomes an issue, you can be combatted with vinegar - vinegar is less of a risk because we don't have a washing machine to take care of. Soap scrum was a big issue for laundry machines.

Q: I'm rinsing for days....
Use less detergent. Vinegar rinses can help cut suds.

Q: What kind of diaper can I handwash?
Flats are best suited for handwashing - they are simple and classic. Looser weave flats like birds eye cotton lend themselves to even easier washing. You can hand wash anything - just expect it to take more time, agititation and experimenting to find the right handle.

Q: I'm using so much water! This can't be good.
Modern washing machines are crazy efficient. Streamline your system, reuse your grey water, and find ways to not run the water. Every parent has a different trick.

Q: Where can I find more help on handwashing?
Look for the Flats & Handwashing Challenge group on Facebook. The event runs every May but the group is open all year. Many parents have great insight.

And yes, you are probably over thinking it.

Q: Do I need to use water softeners when hand washing?
Likely no, many participants from the Flats Challenge report they don't need it for the small loads and handwashing, but some families find it makes a difference. It depends on your detergent, water and technique. Try without and add if needed.

TODDLER CLOTH DIAPERS

Challenges & Questions

Sometimes it feels like all this information is for babies, but it also applies to toddlers, preschoolers and bigger kids.

Biggest Challenges for Toddler Cloth Diapering

Sizing - the term one size diaper is incredibly vague which is why you might feel the struggle when your diapers begin to feel snug around 24-28lbs. But here's a few things I need you to know.

- Some diapers are small and will not last. You'll need to find larger fitting one size diapers or consider size 2 diapers (or size 3).
- The child is in a more chunky phase of their life where they have just experienced rapid weight gain. Many families find when babies turn into toddlers, they slim down and start to fit diapers and clothing better.

Below is two pictures of a 3-year old in a cloth diaper. This child wears a size 4-5, 35 plus pounds, and the diapers still fit. Thats what the last snaps are for. The inserts are small, but they can be adjusted and placed where needed.

Output - newborns pee a little a lot, toddlers pee a lot a little. It can be challenging to find a diaper that can handle large pees at once. In my experience, this kind of flow is best caputred by simple cotton products. But I also have met parents who tackle it using a combo of hemp and microfibre,or bamboo. It's okay to try different things to find a solution.

Try and experiment with different products and combinations. A few of my favourite toddler absorbencies include size 3 cotton prefolds and cotton receieving blankets because they are larger (more surface area), highly absorbent, cheap, and easy to launder. They pair well with other items - wrap a microfibre or hemp inside for even more absorbency.

Yes, you could go with inserts but expect more cost. Find absorbency charts for ideal abosrbency, but most inserts are about 8 ounces of absorbency whether microfibre or bamboo - the biggest change is performance of the material, less the actual absorbency number.

Nighttime diapering - The struggle is capturing a full nights worth of pee with a toddler-sized bladder and longer sleep times. Lucky for you, you can now use more surface area by embracing larger prefolds, flats, or fitted diapers and combo with wool/fleece for stay-dry nights.

- A great addition is a bedwetting mat, like the PeaPod Mat, and adding it to the bed. This waterproof mat is designed to catch pees and can easily be washed. There are many other brands. Mattress pads are expensive, *but of all the products I have bought they are worth every penny. I still use them to catch vomits, nighttime accidents and other bedtime chaos that happens with my six year-old.*

Some families get frustated with **microfibre** during toddlerhood. Microfibre sheds and can become less efficient at holding liquid as it ages. This happens with all textiles but mostly with microfibre.

- Changes in your childs flow and output also make microfibre less ideal for cloth diapering. Consider a natural fibre option.

Potty Training - This is a very unique experience that can change for every family and you may go through different phases of where they want to, don't want to, only poop, hold their bladder and other fun things. Some kids will start at 18 months and some will not be ready until they are 4.

- Follow their lead and, seek out potty training advice that supports your parenting style.
- You will be okay.
- Reusable potty training pants are available but they are not the same as a diaper - they hold significantly less and designed for accidents.

Stinky Diapers - toddler pee and poop is gross and can be hard to wash out. A lot of parents experience shifts in the smells and washing experience at toddlerhood.

- You might need to adjust your wash routine by making small changes to pre-rinses, rinses, water temperature, detergent quantity, or even additives like bleach.

216

Frequently Asked Questions About Toddler Cloth Diapering

Q: My child is 18 months, is it too late to start cloth diapering?

No, it's never too late.

The cost of cloth diapering for a shorter span of time can be more difficult to come to terms with. Some families will have bigger families needing cloth in the future. Keep costs down by purchasing second hand diapers, repurposing materials, and using covers and inserts.

Q: How many diapers does a toddler need in a day?

Toddler or baby, you need to change the diaper regularly. Many families use less diapers during toddlerhood because they hold their bladders longer and pee every 3-4 hours, instead of every 1-2 hours. If the diaper is still dry at two hours, then let it be. You'll learn the groove.

Many toddlers use about 6-8 diapers per day before potty training.

Q: My child is taking off the diaper, what can I do to stop that?

This is a hard phase and many parents struggle. You can try tricks such as putting diapers on backwards, diaper shirts, or tighter pants. In my experience this phase was exploratory and eventually ended.

Q: Help, I have a flooder! My child holds his bladder for hours and then pees one massive flood?

If they aren't developmentally ready for potty training, you can try a variety of diaper strategies. I'm going to be super vague because what works for one person doesn't work for others.

- try microfibre on top, hemp on the bottom and create an absorbency sandwich in a pocket.
- try cotton or bamboo directly against the skin because sometimes liquid doesn't want to move through stay dry layers very easily and that can cause repelling, beading and leaks.
- try a fitted diaper, folded on flat, or folded on prefold - the added surface area can help conquer leaks.
- try wool or fleece covers to contain the leaks.

Q: Toddler poop... I can't handle it....

Toddler poop can be one of the grossest things you will ever experience - especially if they get sick (you can still cloth diaper on medication or if sick). Toddler poop is gross in a disposable and in a cloth diaper.

Things that helped me with toddler poop:
1. Change that diaper ASAP!!! Don't let them sit in poop.
2. Consider liners.
3. You might need to soak it off.
4. Bribe your partner to do the diaper changes.
5. Poops in the diaper are better than the underwear - nobody told me how hard it would be to take off poopy underwear without smearing it.

Ploppable poop is gold - but not everyone will experience it.

Q: I need an overnight diaper that fits my 40lb toddler? Is there an option or is it just size 6 disposables.

Overnight cloth diapers for bigger kids, toddlers or preschoolers or big kids, are harder to source because of their size, speciality and absorbency.

There are products designed for this niche market including Super Undies, Motherease Bedwetters, and sourcing out larger fitting diapers like Snap-EZ (specializes in big kids and adult diapers) paired with larger inserts like large prefolds, inserts or flats.

- Available in pull on options as well as snap-on diapers.
- More expensive product due to product and demand.
- Absorbency makes or breaks the experience. *If you don't have enough textile to catch pee, you're always going to have a leaky mess.*

You can also consider products that are designed to be a size 3 or "bigger" diaper. Many brands will stock these direct from their own online shops or you may find them direct from retailers.

Ask me or a cloth diaper group/blogger/retailer for suggestions because brands are always changing. And you can ask your retailer if they can bring them in for you, they might be able to help you source a product that is difficult to find, or work with you to find a solution.

Q: What are some bigger fitting diapers?

I can think of smaller fitting diapers easier - *Lil Helpers, Rumparooz, Mama Koala, Charlie Banana, AppleCheeks OS, Wink Diapers, Lighthouse Kids Company, and AMP diapers are all diapers that in my experience my child sized out at 32lbs.*

Cloth diapers are sold based on weight categories, but in toddlerhood it's less about the weight and more about the size and shape of the body. Some kids will be 32lbs and fit diapers fine because they have different shaped bodies.

That's where the conversation of having two or three styles or brands in your stash is helpful because there might be a stage where one fits really well and then another stage where the other fits well. Be open to these changes in diapering needs.

You can also find styles that are sold with the term - bigger, plus, super, size 3 - these tend to be diapers that go up to 50lbs and have a larger cut. They may not work with babies under 15-20lbs.

Q: Is there a style or type of cloth diaper that fits bigger?

Generally, covers fit larger than pockets or all in one diapers. All in one cloth diapers tend to be smaller fitting, but that's not always the rule.

Q: My child wont sit still for a diaper change?

Give them something to do like a toy they can only play with. Talk to them about what is going on - tell them what you are doing, why you are doing it, and each step. You will feel a little funny talking to your-self but it helps make diaper changes easier.

And you can also try changing standing up - I believe this is also known as a Montessori diaper change. Difficult, but not impossible.

NIGHTTIME DIAPERING
How to get started

Cloth diapering at night can be challenging. It makes wash routines seem simple. Why? Capturing nighttime pee - 8-12 hours - in a cloth diaper can be bulky, expensive, and cumbersome.

Younger babies might need to be changed throughout the night (even in disposable diapers). They quickly outpee diapers for their size, they poop in the night, or just fuss.

Many families use disposable diapers at night. That is okay. You are still a cloth diaper parent. This is an easy way to ensure you have a dry morning. It can be more cost efficient. It is okay to do a mix of diapering. Don't let anyone tell you otherwise.

These are reinforced fleece pants from Baby Koala specifically designed as an alternative diaper cover - but fleece PJ's also act as a good buffer

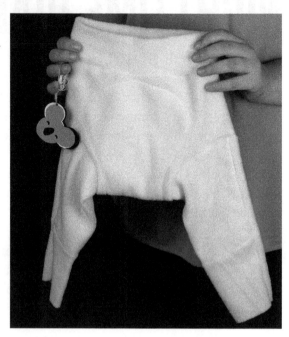

If you want to start cloth diapering at night: trial and error. What works for one family might not work for you.

Please don't get caught up in the terms heavy wetter, super soaker, nigthtime diaper. It is marketing hype and there is no industry standard. Each brand and person has a different opinion.

Words of Encouragment

1. Before trial and error, make sure you have a mattress protector.

2. Try using fleece PJ's as a buffer to reduce wetness on the sheets.

3. If you can afford it, try wool covers because it does act better than fleece and can absorb up to 30% of it's weight in liquid.

4. Not every kid is a heavy wetter super soaker at night. Don't let the conversation of expensive fitteds get you down - that might not be your story, but you wont know until you try.

5. You totally got this - it's normal for something to work one night and not the other.

Easy Nighttime Cloth Diapers

- **Upcycled cotton t-shirts or receiving blankets** - these items can hold 12-20 oz of absorbency. This is a cheap and accessible way to start nighttime diapering without purchasing anything.

  Simply fold these items into a pad and stuff into pocket or a cover.

- **Nighttime prefolds** - 3ply prefold diapers or those marketed specifically for nights offer 12-18oz of absorbency. This is a good middle ground for most children. A prefold diaper offers a lower cost per ounce than fitted diapers and can easily be padfolded into a pocket diaper without much bulk (about the same as two micro-fibre inserts) If these do not have enough absorbency, pair them with a hemp insert for more boost.

  Simply padfold and add to a pocket or cover, or even all in one.

- **Nighttime All In One diapers** - you can find all in one diapers sold specifically for nights, these offer anywhere from 10-15 oz of absorbency (sometimes more). They are a good choice for light wetters but many super soakers may outpace them.

  In my experience these products are not good for true heavy wetters who need 20+ ounces of absorbency unless paired with additional boosters.

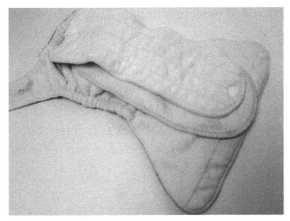

Remember, heavy wetter or nighttime diaper is an unregulated term based on generalizations.

This is a popular overnight AIO diaper - it wasn't enough absorbency so I added an hemp booster to the diaper. I like hemp in this situation because it's trim and slowly caputres compression from the top layers.

- **Fitted Diapers** - this is an easy purchase for overnight cloth diapering and there are lots of makes and models from cheap to expensive with a variety of experiences. I know, right?

I don't recommend cheap fitted diapers for super soakers because the absorbency has been subpar in my experience.

Unfortunatley, the cost of a product does increase with absorbency. You just can't get 20-30 ounces of absorbency with less than $10 of material. This is a conversation that many seamstresses and brands have discussed on the podcast.

Fitted diaper absorbency can vary from 18-25 ounces for standard styles, with products exceeding 30 ounces. They are significantly more expensive with brands like Lilly & Frank exceeding $40-50 per diaper. This is beause of the absorbency, craftsmanship and overall product quality. Many of these diapers can hold over 25 ounces and will be suitable for super soakers.

If you need a diaper that will work in a unique situation reach out to the maker for support. Also many of these big Work At Home Mom brands that make custom-designed diapers also have buy and sell groups where you can find used products at a lower cost.

I have podcasts about overnight diapering with Eco Accountrements, Pooters, CooperRose, and Lilly & Frank that might be insightful in learning more about these brands and overnight fitted diapers.

- **Inserts & More** - you can use a mash-up of different inserts to create an all-time nighttime diaper. Combine bamboo, hemp, cotton inserts, flats and prefolds to create something that works for your child.

On Instagram, I have learnt of many incredible combinations that I wouldn't have considered. So start with what you have and make the magic happen with your own trial and error. If two inserts leak, try a third, if it's too bulky and dry, try a booster or smaller insert. You can swap out products from different brands to make a winning night combo without purchasing new products.

Yo, make friends with your retailer if you are struggling to find a combo that works. Be honest about your budget, and say "I have tried this and this, and this was my experience, I could probably spend $10 ... what do you think would make it right?"

So many retailers and parents are on social media, we want to help you.

I want you to know: we can help you, but we need to know the story of what you tried, what you're willing to try, and if you have any limitations (budget, baby size, washing, drying, etcetera).

Many of you want to know the right way to layer the inserts depending on textile, but I want to reinforce that every textile brand performs different for each child. The diagram below is an ideal, it might change depending on your needs.

- Avoid hemp as your top layer if you have a flooder (lots of pee all at once) and avoid as your top layer if you don't have a barrier to the skin. Everything else is trial and error. You can do this.

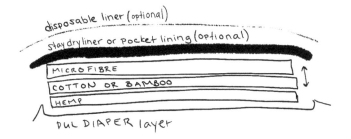

Still Struggling to find something that works?

Reach out for 1:1 support to find a cloth diaper combo for nights that will work for your family.

When connecting with someone - talk about what you've tried, where you want to go, and what your budget is. This will help others on the internet provide an answer that works for you.

I also recommend looking at absorbency lists that parents have created. I have a list, All About Cloth Diapers has a list, and so do many other cloth diaper bloggers to represent the diverse types of products on the market. Compare what you have tried to the list, and then what you think might need to achieve your goal.

Absorbency lists aren't perfect and represent ideal experiences. You might have a different experience.

But say you tried THIS Insert + THAT Insert, and the list suggests, 4 ounces + 7 ounces, and you want to find something that's trimmer, or cheaper, you can look for a product with 10-12 ounces and try that.

Or if you destroyed a fitted diaper, 12 ounces, and someone recommends ABC brand All In One Diaper, you can cross reference and see that others experienced only 10 ounces of absorbency. Maybe that's not a great choice for you - or maybe it is if you paired it with a hemp insert that added an extra 5 ounces.

Frequently Asked Questions About Night Cloth Diapering

Q: My child keeps waking up in the night? Could it be my cloth diaper? Should I be using stay dry?
Maybe? That is a very one-to-one experience.

In my experience, the sensation of peeing was enough to wake up my child. My child did not sleep through the night until he could hold his bladder. I am team you gotta experiment with this one. If your child sleeps through the night in a disposable and that's important to you, then do that.

Q: How many night diapers do I need?
One for every night before wash day, plus one. There will be that night they poop before bed and you have to change their diaper. Better to be prepared if you can. If you wash every third day - you might want 3 night diapers.

Q: Is nighttime cloth diapering expensive?
Only if you want it to be expensive. You can use an XL cotton t-shirt, upcycle an old wool sweater for a low-cost night cloth diaper. You can choose to purchase second hand cloth diapers or repurpose other products to work for night.

It doesn't have to be a fancy fitted diaper or marketed product. Night cloth diapering is only expensive if you want it to be.

Q: Only my night diapers smell?! Help
Nighttime urine can build up in a diaper. Try rinsing your diapers every morning and letting them dry out. To get them clean again, try a strip or a heavy wash cycle with hot water. If using expensive fitteds, consult with the brand for the best 1:1 recommendation.

Q: Is every night diaper bulky?
No. Night diapers can be a little bulky, especially on smaller children but they don't have to be bulky. Some night diapers are really trim based on the fold, quality of the textile, and the absorbency needs of the child.

Q: Is bulk bad or uncomfortable?
No. Most children will be just fine and adjust accordingly.

Mr. Bear is wearing a t-shirt diaper. You can use any old natural fibre t-shirt as a diaper in a pinch. If it absorbs it works

Q: I have a tummy sleeper...

Add more absorbency to the front of the diaper by folding it where it needs to go. You might also benefit from a diaper that has a front elastic along the waist snaps.

Q: Is hemp the best diaper?

No. Hemp will not solve all your problems. Hemp is best used along with other materials to compliment and create a great cloth diapering experience. But, what's more important is finding something that performs and is in your budget.

I don't want you going out buying a hemp diaper for nights just because it's "the most absorbent" textile. Instead, I want you to make a thoughtful decision based on your needs as a consumer, and price point to work for you.

Q: Fitted diapers that wont break the bank?

Ahhhh - buy used? Cheap fitted diapers can result in poor cloth diaper experiences (shrink, poor fit, lack of absorbency). I recommend trying a prefold or flat diaper for a comparable absorbency for a lower cost, easier to wash, more accessible cloth diaper choice.

Start where you are.
Use what you have.
Do what you can.

– Arthur Ashe

YOU CAN DO THIS
There is no wrong way to cloth diaper.

If baby's bum is happy and healthy then you're doing it right.
If you're happy and healthy then you're doing it right.

If you get leaks, we all get leaks.
If you get rashes, that happens.
If you get smells, that happens sometimes.
If you're struggling, then ask for help.

You can cloth diaper full time or part time.

You can cloth diaper on the weekend and disposable diaper during the week.

You can take a break from cloth diapering and come back when life settles.

You can hire out your laundry and employ a cloth diaper service.

How you cloth diaper doesn't have to be PERFECT every time. Cloth diapering is a unique journey for every person and family. You are a cloth diaper mom whether you cloth diaper once a day or full time. Don't let anyone tell you are not.

We are allowed grace for the imperfections in our life.
You don't need to apologize for it.

COMMON FAQ

These are all the things that don't fit neatly into other sections of this book. Lots of travel related things.

Q: What do I do with diapers between babies for storage?
Make sure your diapers don't have any build up or excess detergent by giving them a quick wash or rinse before storing. You want to store clean diapers.

Most brands will recommend storing diapers in a cool ventilated space. It's recommended that they have space to breathe. This includes a cardboard box, or even a Rubbermaid. It's not recommended to vacuum seal cloth diapers but check with your brand for a rec.

Elastics can dry rot with time - if you are planning on storing for many years, you might sell your stash and purchase a new one. You might consider keeping prefolds, but passing covers and pockets onto a friend. Sometimes storage situations do go wrong. Just a risk to think about. I've seen those stories.

Q: Can I travel with cloth diapers?
Yes! You can travel with cloth diapers. You can fly with them, road trip, or any other adventure.

Q: How do I wash my diapers somewhere else?
Just start. A few bad washes will not ruin your diapers and you can reset them afterwards. I would try your routine when you get there and if they feel a little funky make small changes.

For example, my moms house has really soft water so my diapers feel like slime when I pull them out of the machine. I have to remember to use less detergent and an extra rinse to get all the suds out. It is a learning curve but this is where knowing the reasons behind and being prepared to problem solve yourself will be your greatest strength. And I know that you are wise and capable of making these decisions.

Q: Can I take cloth diapers camping?
Yes! I love taking flats and handwashing, or I will bring enough for the trip and wash when I get home.

Q: What about biodegradable inserts?
Another great product for travel and camping, or at home. GroVia, and maybe Flip, make different types of disposable inserts. Some of them can be composted and some can't.

I like to disposable inserts them when I go on a hiking trip as my back up diaper because I didn't want to carry a bulky diaper so instead I would have an insert and cover in the bag.

Q: How do I get my partner on board?
Open and honest conversations about why you want to do this. Share truthful information that helps them understand and work through the myths they beliveve. It might take them time.

They might never like it.

On the podcast, most of the parents say that exposure and real life practice of cloth diapering brings partners around. Take time, be patient with them, and stand your ground about why it's important to you.

Q: The people in my life are unsupportive of my decision to cloth diaper...
Do you need their approval to cloth diaper?

A lot of the times, other people are influenced by decades of disposable diaper marketing and myths of cloth diapering. They have misconceptions and you'll need to approach each person with a different strategy.

Some people will be open to learning and some people will not. Some people will fight you no matter what.
Pick your battles and remember that you are not responsible for them loving cloth diapers. Some people will just not get it, and that's okay.

Q: Can I use cloth diapers at my childcare facility?
Maybe. There are very few legal rules to prevent you from cloth diapering at a childcare facility. Many parents send cloth diapers to daycare with their kids and all is good.

Some parents face challenges with cloth diapering at a facility and this is really going to be unique to each person. Remember that we all carry our own stories and experiences. I would recommend looking for my podcast episode on cloth diapering at daycare. These stories share some great support to help you find your daycare groove.

- You will need to provide a full day or two of diapers.
- Most care facilities will not swap out inserts, so it will need to be an entire diaper change.
- You might need to provide a bag for each diaper change.
- You might need to provide instructions.
- You might need to label your diaper using a sticker, or a snap-on.
- You might consider snap blockers to block off the snaps that they shouldn't use.
- If they are not familiar with cloth diapers, you might need to send them a list showing them how to do it and what to do. The learning curve is hard but you can help make it easier.
- Many parents will have enough diapers for a week, and then wash once a week. Some will wash every few days.
- Find a routine that works for you and live it.
- Be okay with making mistakes, needing disposables, and taking breaks.

Q: My doctor says cloth diapers are bad, or unhealthy.
Ask them about that? Keep asking questions because they are likely perceiving a few bad experiences; maybe they had patients with bad wash routines and chronic rashes or they hated cloth diapering.

Ask questions and for research - it's most likely a personal opinion.

Q: My friend says the water consumption of cloth diaper laundry is no better than disposables. Is that true?
Maybe. It's all really variable. And there are so many pieces to the story line of cloth diapering and laundry that it is hard to tell. It really depends on the story you want to tell. That's the fun thing about stats

- we can use words to tell different stories.

You don't need to convince them to cloth diaper. You need to cloth diaper for you and be true in the reasons why you choose to cloth diaper.

Q: Bailey what do you think about this brand? Is it good?
Maybe? Good is variable and in my time as a blogger and cloth diaper content creator I have learnt that we all have different experiences with products. I gave recommendations throughout this book but that's based on my limited experience with products.

A product might be good, but you will not know until you try. I would encourage you to follow the cookie crumbs of the cloth diaper journey. Try that brand, ask that brand questions, and be willing to fall in love.

My experience with a product is not the only one, and I'm aware of that and want you to also be aware. Check out my blog for reviews and different recommendations at www.simplymombailey.com

Help! What about this unique scenario that isn't in this book!?
Reach out to me for additional support or questions. Find a Facebook Group and ask for different ideas and strategies - I recommend the group - All About Cloth Diapers Chat - but you can find one that is a local based, or brand based, or just fits you better.

Check my blogs - www.simplymombailey.com or www.clothdiaperpodcast.com - because both of those places I have written a ton of cloth diaper reviews and guides to different situations including newborn diapering, overnight diapers, toddler diapers, cloth diapering 2 under 2, and more. But, we are many many pages into this book and I wanted to give you the basics to feel empowered and ready to start cloth diapering.

The Cloth Diaper Podcast is a podcast sharing stories of cloth diapering from parents, cloth diaper brands and retailers from around the world. We talk about the many unique cloth diapering experiences, problems and help share stories to build community.

Listen to the Podcast on your favourite Podcast application (available on Apple Podcasts, Spotify, YouTube, PodBean, and more) or online at www.clothdiaperpodcast.com.

OTHER RESOURCES
Videos, creators, and groups

Jacqueline - @OfficialJaysNest
This YouTuber is a great resource for in-depth video content on cloth diapering including reviews and recommendations.

YouTube: https://www.youtube.com/jaysnest

Kaitlin - @ModernBottomBabies
This blogger is a great resource for simple cloth diapering, newborn cloth diapering and motherhood. Find her on Instagram.

Website: www.modernbottombabies.com

Jennifer - @AllAboutClothDiapers
If you're looking for a supportive group with sound wash routine advice, visit the All About Cloth Diaper Chat group on Facebook. Jennifer has great many resources to solve laundry battles.

@HonestToCloth
This UK based mama has a great Instagram and blog if you're looking for more euro-centric cloth diapering support including simple Instagram posts and video content.

Website: www.honesttoclothcom.wordpress.com

There are many more cloth diaper blogs and resources online. I share lots of this on my Facebook and Instagram account.

And don't forget me! I also have a YouTube Channel:
https://www.youtube.com/clothdiaperpodcast

and you can find support on Instagram @ClothDiaperPodcast

or on my websites: www.simplymombailey.com
or www.clothdiaperpodcast.com.

GLOSSARY OF TERMS

Absorbency: refers to materials that absorb liquid in a diaper this can include sewn in soaker pads, inserts, doublers, and other materials. Absorbency is also referenced in terms of quantity about how much absorbency a product has.

Absorbency testing: the act of checking how much liquid a material holds by pouring water over it, or soaking it in water and calculating how many fluid ounces it held. These numbers can vary, but can help provide insight to comparing products.

Adjusted: a term used for fitted diapers in other parts of the world.

AIO: All In One cloth diaper (this cloth diaper is everything you need to get started it has a water resistant exterior and sewn in absorbent inner).

AI2: All In Two cloth diaper (the idea of this cloth diaper is that it can be two types of diapers and be used like a cover, pocket, or even All In One in style. It might have a pocket, it might have snap in inserts. There is no solid industry standard on this definition).

Aplix: a brand of hook and loop fastener used on diapers.

Bamboo: a processed natural fibre used in cloth diaper textiles. It is typically blended with cotton or hemp.

BAIO: Bamboo All In One Diaper (commonly referring to the Nicki's Diapers version, but others exist).

Birds eye: a type of cotton textile with a unique texture that looks like birds eye squares.

Blow out: when a diaper leaks, specifically poop related.

Boingo: a diaper fastener about 2 inches long with claws on both end. Sold in a two pack.

Booster: a smaller insert added to a cloth diaper to boost the absorbency of the diaper, typically less than 5 ounces.

Borax: laundry additive used as a softener, but considered to be harsh for diapers.

Brick & Mortar: a physical store.

Bullet Proof: used when talking about night time cloth diapers that do not leak.

CBI: charcoal bamboo inserts (charcoal bamboo is used as a colouring agent to give micro fleece a darker colour).

CD - cloth diaper

Cheapies: slang used to refer to cheap cloth diapers purchased from overseas wholesalers at bulky pricing and without warranty or additional support.

Cloth Wipes: small pieces of material used to clean bums in the same manner as a disposable wipe. Use with water or a solution. Washed with diapers.

CPSIA: Child product safety improvement act responsible for compliance testing and certification of baby products such as cloth diapers.

Coconut Oil: is a natural occurring oil used to treat rashes and for skin health. It is safe to use with cloth diapers and washes out.

Compression: when weight is added to a diaper and this can either encourage absorption of liquid or encourage liquid to squeeze out of a product and leak out gaps in the diaper. Typical compression is the squeeze of a diaper shirt (onesie) on a diaper or a child sitting on a diaper in a chair, carseat, or baby carrier.

Contour Diapers: simple hourglass shaped diapers like a fitted cloth diaper without snaps or hook and loop.

Cotton: a natural fibre used in cloth diapers. It is cheap and absorbent. It comes in many forms, including bleached, unbleached and organic.

Cover: a diaper cover made of water resistant material. There are covers with snaps made out of PUL, or fleece, or wool, or other.

Cloth Diaper Retailer: an online store or physical location that sells cloth diapers; typically by signing wholesale contracts with cloth diaper brands.

Diaper Pod: a small 3D carrying case for diapers. It is a pod shape, usually designed to hold diapers standing upright.

Diaper Service: businesses that provide and/or wash cloth diapers for parents. Usually pick up and return direct to your home.

Diaper Sprayer: a device attached to the toilet that uses pressurized water to spray poop off.

Disposable Inserts: inserts designed to be used with cloth diapers that can then be thrown away. Some are biodegradable.

Delaminating: when the lamination applied to make PUL begins to separate from the textile creating bubbles or peeling.

Doubler: an insert added to a cloth diaper to double the absorbency.

Double Gusset: typically defined as a second set of leg elastics.

EBF: exclusively breast fed.

EC: elimination communication (a style of diapering responding a child's needs to urinate or defecate by taking them to the potty at a young age).

Edge Wear: when the fibres begin to break down along the edge causing holes.

EO: essential oils (proceed with caution around infants and babies).

Fairy: someone who buys diapers with the intent to send them to someone else. People fairy diapers when diapers are only available at a certain location or event but sought by someone who cannot be there.

Family Cloth: using reusable wipes for toilet paper.

Fasteners: fasteners hold flats, prefolds, and some fitted diapers together. There typically have prongs or teeth to dig into the

Cloth Diaper Acronyms are similar to other acronyms used by other communities. Don't hesitate to ask for Clarification of terminology to understand. Many brands have different definitions of design features and terms. Terminology changes.

fabric. Popular fasteners include: boingo, snappi, diaper pin, diaper belts.

F&C: Free and clean (a type of detergent).

Felted: the process of wool weave tightening. This happens with agitation and heat to knit blends of wool; usually by accident.

Fitted Diaper: This is an absorbent piece of material in a diaper shape with some sort of fastener. It is only absorbent material (hemp, cotton, bamboo) and you need a cover to keep clothing dry.
FF: formula fed

Flat: simple, single layer sheet of absorbent material typically a square and can be made out of hemp, cotton or bamboo.

Fleece: a synthetic material with a soft fuzzy touch. It comes in many forms, regular, micro, and polar. It can be stay dry; thinner products more suited for diapers.

Fluff: nickname terminology used within the cloth diaper community. Commonly used as "fluff bums" "fluff mail" and other.

Fluff Mail: cloth diaper mail.

FTM: first time mom.

FST: flour sack towel (cheap kitchen towels made our of 100% cotton available at stores like Walmart or Target and other).

Grab Bags - bundles of products, sometimes seconds quality, sometimes unsold product, sold at a lower post.

HE: high efficiency, refers to appliances like washing machines and their ability to perform using less water or electricity.

Heavy Wetter: terminology used to define a child who out pees a diaper within a two hour window. There is no industry standard. In my experience, a daytime heavy wetter needs 10+ ounces of natural fibre absorbency during the day and 20+ ounces at night.

Hemp: a natural fibre material used in cloth diaper inserts. It is typically blended with cotton or bamboo, and in ratios of 40-60%.

Hip Snap: additional snap on the wing of the diaper, located about one inch in from the edge, intended to hold the diaper at the wing and prevent wing droop.

Hook & Loop/ H&L: a type of closure made popular by the brand Velcro™.

Hybrid: This type of cloth diaper can sometimes be referred to as an AI2 diaper and is typically a cloth diaper cover with snaps. Sometimes a cloth diaper will be called a hybrid if it can be used with disposable diaper inserts.

Hybrid Fitted Diaper: This is a fitted cloth diaper with an inner layer of water resistant material to reduce wetness through the exterior of the diaper.

Insert: the absorbent part of the diaper. Anything can be an insert with the most popular ones being made out of Microfibre or cotton.

Lanolin: a natural wax obtained recreated by sheep and used to boost the water resistant performance of wool or fleece products. Lanolin is used to waterproof fleece or wool diaper covers and is naturally antibacterial.

Laundry Tabs: additional pieces of hook & loop added to the diaper so that the sticky part of the hook & loop can be fastened to itself for wash. If left unattached, hook & loop can snag other textiles.

Liner: cloth or disposable layer of material used in a diaper for easy clean up of solid waste; typically made of fleece for stay dry benefits.

Liniment: a natural cream product use to clean baby bums that protects and heals the skin.

LO: Little One.

MF/Microfibre: Microfibre is a synthetic textile used in diaper inserts because of its absorbency and can't be put against the skin.

Micro Fleece: a soft fuzzy synthetic material. Micro fleece is very thin. Used as a stay dry material for cloth diapers.

Microseude: a dense synthetic textile that is soft and smooth. It is used as a stay dry material.

Minky: a synthetic fleece material similar to polar fleece used as exterior of a cloth diaper.

Modern Cloth Nappy (MCN):

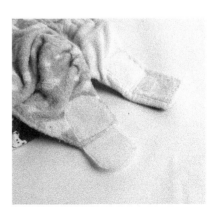

this term is commonly used in Australia to refer to cloth diapers.

Nappy: another term for diaper used in other parts of the world.

Natural Fibres: textiles made from cotton, hemp, or bamboo. (is a heavily process natural fibre). Can be put against the skin.

NCDR: not cloth diaper related (term used in online cloth diaper communities).

Newborn (nb): specifically sized diapers designed for babies under 12 to 15lbs.

OBF: organic bamboo fleece.

OBV: organic bamboo velour, a plush knit.

OS, One Size: a term used to describe diapers that can be adjusted to fit babies from 8 to 35lbs. This range fits most from birth to potty training.

OT: off topic (used in online communities when the conversation is a different topic than the defined niche).

OTB: on the bum, diapers on the child.

Padfold: the art of folding absorbency into a simple pad shape similar to an insert (3-4" by 5-7").

Plastic Pants: old school vinyl diaper covers

Pocket: a pocket cloth diaper has an pocket opening between the inner liner and water resistant exterior. The absorbent insert goes in the middle.

Pilling: a natural process when fibres begin to ball up. This happens in the wash to fleece, velours, hook&loop, and other textiles.

Prefold: a absorbent material using 4-8 layers of gauze folded into rectangle and sewn in place. Typically a prefold has three sections with a middle section double the thickness of the sides). Prefolds are folded

PreFlat: is similar to a prefold in that it is 2-3 layers of material sewn into a shape, but typically features wings to easily wrap and fasten

Prepping: the act of preparing cloth diapers for use by washing them until they have become absorbent. Synthetic fibres like Microfibre, microfleece, and bamboo only need to be washed once or twice, while other natural fibres like hemp and cotton need to be washed 3-5 times (sometimes more depending on the brand). To see if your product is ready to be used poor a stream of water onto the product and if it absorbs your good to go. Some items like micro fleece and Microfibre might need compression to absorb.

PUL: polyurethane laminate (type of water resistant material used in diaper construction)

Repelling: a term used when cloth diapers no longer absorb liquids. This can occur with build up of detergent or fabric softener. Some materials do need compression to absorb adequately.

Rise: the length of a diaper that is adjusted using snaps or elastics.

RLR: a laundry treatment process to remove mineral build up from textiles.

Ruffles: ruffle elastics have serged edges and a distinct ruffle pattern.

SAHM/P/D: stay at home mom/parent/dad

Serged Edges: a stitching technique applied to the raw edge of a material. It is loops of thread to prevent fraying.

Silk: a natural fibre used in cloth diapering. Raw silk has a natural anti-inflammatory effect and cools the skin. Used short term, and hand washed.

Sized: a term used to describe diapers that fit a certain size; sized diapers don't typically adjust.

Size 1, 2, 3: diapers designed to fit a limited size range.

Stripping: the act of removing build up detergent or minerals from diapers. There are many different ways to strip diapers. Stripping should not be your first line of defense when troubleshooting diapers and can he hard on diapers. Frequent stripping is not normal.

Stalking: the act of actively waiting and seeking out a diaper or product to release.

Stocking: an event when diapers list on a website at a specific time and date. Stockings are sometimes used with brands with limited product.

sposie: slang used by parents to refer to disposable diapers.

Snappi: a three pronged diaper fastener available in two sizes.

Soaker: a type of insert, typically referred to a long insert that is folded in half or thirds to fit into a diaper. Soakers are often associated with fitted cloth diapers.

Softeners: laundry additives used to soften hard water to increase detergent efficiency.

Stash: the term used to describe a collection of cloth diapers.

Stay Dry: the idea that a material wicks away moisture to the absorbency underneath quickly preventing a wet feeling against baby's bum. The most common stay dry is microfleece, but other products provide a similar experience: raw silk, fleece, athletic wicking jersey.

Swim Diapers: diaper specifically designed for swimming.

Sunning Diapers: the process of putting diapers in the sun to remove stains.

Trifold: a rectangle 2-3 layer insert that is folded into thirds and used as an insert.

Tummy Panel: a layer of PUL on the inside front of a diaper to prevent wicking at the front.

TPU: thermal polyurethane laminate (a type of PUL, all TPU is PUL). This process is done with

heat bonding instead of a chemical process.

TTO: tea tree oil.

Turned & Top Stitch: The elastics have been encased and top-stitch. There is no ruffle, or exposed thread.

Velcro: a trademark owned version of hook & loop.

WAHM - Work At Home Mom

Wash Routine: the routine for washing diapers that is unique to each person. There is no one wash routine but only guidelines and suggestions to help you clean your diapers.

Wet Bag: a small reusable bag made out of water resistant material used to store dirty diapers.

Wet Pail: no longer recommended due to a health and safety hazard, but previous generations soaked diapers in a water until wash day.

Wicking: the transfer of moisture from the one spot to another. Typically used in reference to wicking with diapers were the diaper transfers moisture to clothes.

Wipe Solution: liquid used to

moisten cloth wipes, DIY or
store purchased

Wool: a natural fibre material
used in cloth diapering because
of it's absorbency properties.
Wool can hold up to 30% of it's
weight in moisture. Some wool
can be machine washed, but
mostly hand washed. Needs to
be lanolized to be water resistant. Wool can be used as a stay
dry liner.

Woolies: slang used for wool
clothing, specifically bottoms.

Wool Wash: detergent/soap
specifically for wool products. It
is typically gentle, no-rinse.

Wrap: type of cloth diaper
cover; typically larger fitting
product intended for folded
flats and fitted diapers.

Zinc: zinc oxide is an ingredient in diaper rash ointments.
It is used to heal rashes. Zinc is
safe for cloth diapers but may
cause staining.

BUY & SELL TERMS

These are terms you might see in buy & sell spaces online. They are commonly used, some are dated.

BN: Brand New diaper, should still be in package or unprepped.

BST: Buy, Sell, Trade - this term is used in reference to the act of buying/selling/trading diapers or to a refer to a group that is dedicated to buying/selling/trading diapers.

Bump: to comment on a post with the intent of bumping it to the top of the group/page.

Cheapies: diapers purchased online at low cost. Each group defines cheapies differently; most are worried about buying and selling diapers without compliant testing or responsible manufacturing.

Destash: the process of selling off a cloth diaper stash for whatever reason.

DC#: Delivery Confirmation Number

DISO: desperately in search of

EMT: electric money transfer. Not recommended as there is no buyer protection.

ETA: edited to add.

EUC: Excellent Used Condition (ideally a diaper in this condition has strong like new elastics, no flaws, and minimally used for less than a year)

Feedback: some websites have feedback groups/pages where you can leave and read feedback about a buyer or seller's previous experiences.

FFS: free for shipping; you pay shipping costs for a product.

FPP: Funded PayPal

FRB: flat rate box; a product purchased at the post office that ships for a flat rate cost.

FBE: Flat rate envelope; a product purchased to shipping that comes with a flat rate cost.

FS: for sale

FSO: for sale only (not open to trades)

FSOT: for sale or trade

FT: for trade

GN: gender neutral

Good Elastics: elastics stil have bounce in them, similar to new condition but can be used without impacting size and fit of the diaper.

GUC: Good Used Condition (this diaper likely has been used in a stash longer than a year, and elastics might be beginning to go, but shouldn't. There shouldn't be any flaws besides cosmetic)

IHA: I have available; typically used when searching for trades or for sale.

ISO: In Search Of or looking for.

LM: Letter mail (lettermail shipping is uninsured shipping method in Canada where a package can be sent for the price of a letter if it's the size of a letter)

LN: Like New (likely used just once or twice)

Minor Staining: Diapers have faded stains that may or may not have been treated. Not super visible in photos, but evident in real life.

MMAO: make me an offer

Next: next in line

NIP: new in package (hasn't been removed from the original packaging since purchasing)

NOOP: new out of package; is out of package, but has not been washed.

NWOT: new without tags (never been washed but tags are no long attached or available)

NWT: New With Tags, is a diaper that is new and still has tags attached or is still in the package.

OS: one size (typically 8-35lbs)

OTW - on the way

Play Condition: diaper is in bad shape, may have use defects.

PM: personal message (sent a message)

PPD: postage paid domestic postage is included in the price)

PP: PayPal; preferred payment method for online cloth diaper sales. Do not use friends & family, but rather request money or invoices for service/good. This will offer buyer/seller protection

247

should a problem arise.

Relaxed Elastics: elastics are close to being replaced, but still have some bounce in them. The elastics likely have 6-12 months of life yet. They are usually an inch longer than new.

Seconds: diapers with cosmetic flaws that are not good enough for retail. They are sold at a reduced priced because of these flaws. Usually market with a crossed tag.

VGUC: very good condition (somewhere between excellent and good used condition)

UC: used condition.

CLOTH DIAPER BRANDS

AACD - All About Cloth Diapers (Website/Group)
AC - AppleCheeks
BB - Best Bottom
BG - bumGenius
CB - Charlie Banana, Cotton Babies
CDP - Cloth Diaper Podcast
DJ - Diaper Junction
FB - FuzziBunz
FLU - Fluff Love University (cloth diaper school of thought)
GB - Geffen Baby
GCDC - Great Cloth Diaper Change, annual event
GV - GroVia
GMD - Green Mountain Diapers
HH - Happy Heiny's
LFP - Little Fanny Pants
LHK - Lighhtouse Kids Company
LPO - La Petite Ourse
ME - Mother-ease
MK - MamaKoala
PC - Petite Crown
RAR - Rumparooz
SB - Smart Bottoms or SoftBums
SSB - Sustainablebabyish
TT - Twinkie Tush

Index

Hey, that's me! I'm thrilled you've taken the jump to trust me as a source for the basics on cloth diapering.

My name is Bailey Bouwman. I'm a cloth diaper mom and educator. I have been blogging about cloth diapering since 2015. I graduated from the University of Northern British Columbia with a Bachelor of Arts in Environmental Studies in 2014, and earned my certificate in Public Relations from Ryerson University. When I'm not talking about cloth diapering, I'm a social media strategist and communications assistant in Northern BC working with small businesses on Public Relations, blogging, or putting thoughts into action.

I believe cloth diapering is about the collective wisdom of our communities and support peer to peer sharing of knowledge. I recognize what works for me might not work for you. As is everything in motherhood. This is not a space of science; it's a space of community-based wisdom. With that I acknowledge the many women and people before me who have built this community to what it is today. This isn't new information. This is me collecting all that I know from all the corners of the world and bringing it into one easy guide to help you out.

Welcome to my cloth diaper space! Come and join the community online. Share your experience, speak your story, and let's support one another in achieving their goals.

Always,
Bailey

Living and working on the unceded territory
of the Lheidli T'enneh in Northern British Columbia